THE EFFECTIVE BOARD MEMBER

WHAT EVERY BOARD MEMBER SHOULD KNOW

KARL GEORGE MBE

Testimonials

"So often we assume corporate governance to be a daunting set of rules, a system for leadership and control in our organisations, something done *to* us by our executives and risk control teams. I came away from the EBM Programme with a fundamental understanding that governance defines the central nervous system of our organisations. With a phenomenal depth of knowledge steeped in history, Karl helped us develop an ethical mind-set; giving us tools that would help our organisations and people take healthy risk and innovate whilst protecting us from damaging failure.

Even as junior traders at UBS in 2007, this programme would have empowered us to find a new way and ultimately protect us from our failure in 2011. To successfully rebuild our social contracts in a world where trust between our societies and their institutions is at historical lows, Karl's EBM programme is a powerful tool for all our people – not just our board members and executives."

Kweku Adoboli - Culture and Systems Advisor, Public Speaker, Former Trader at UBS Global Synthetic Equities

"I attended 4 days of training for the Effective Board Member Programme delivered by Mr Karl George. The volume of information, forms, examples, and cases we have from our marvellous instructor make us extremely Effective Board Members and can add lots of value to the board and organisation. I recommend each board member to attend that programme and feel for himself the added value he will gain."

Marwan H. Alkhouli, FGP,CPA,CFE,CRP,CRA,CBM,CPM,CICA,CFC, General Manager – Head of Operations Group at Oman Arab Bank

"I've attended many courses all over the world – in the US, Europe and the Far East. This Effective Board Member course is the best course I've attended within only two days, and which I've benefitted from more than any other course within that duration in my life."

Osama Alahdal, Saudi Airlines PwC - EBM Programme Graduate

"Governance is the system of rules, practices and processes by which an organisation is directed and controlled. An effective board will provide good governance and leadership by understanding its role and responsibilities; behaving with integrity, openness and accountability; and making decisions that are effective, inclusive and transparent.

The governance and management of sports organisations has, in recent years, increasingly come under the spotlight and the programmes that Karl George MBE runs are an excellent way for current and future board members to learn the practicalities of achieving good governance in a sporting environment."

Richard Bevan, Chief Executive at the League Managers' Association

"I cannot imagine anyone more passionate about corporate governance than The Governor, Karl George. His effervescent 'tingly' style of delivery makes the Effective Board Member Programme and now this book, a joy to experience.

Karl truly makes the often dry but hugely important subject of corporate governance engaging. Now, more than ever, organisations and their individual board members need to understand fully the obligations they are under, and how effective corporate governance can and will help drive their businesses forwards. *The Effective Board*

Member is a really accessible guide for anyone in a board position or aspiring to be so."

Alex Bishop, Partner and National Head of Dispute Resolution & Compliance at Shoosmiths LLP

"Karl has a practical and down-to-earth style, which he brings to everything he does. This book is very useful reading for anyone wanting a successful career as a board director."

Bridget Blow CBE, former Bank of England Director

"Karl George has designed an easy-to-grasp approach to corporate governance, which wins the buy-in of directors with a wide range of experience. His no-nonsense style is perfect for the aspiring director who wants to know how best to face the new responsibilities of the boardroom. His style and engaging manner are perfect as a refresher for directors who are facing changing economic and political environments in the business they have served for some time. I would use Karl's knowledge and skills in any sector. His new book is a worthy text for anyone anticipating getting to grips with good governance."

Suzy Brain England OBE, Chair of Doncaster & Bassetlaw Teaching Hospitals Trust, Chair of Derwent Housing Association, Chair of Sheffield Business Improvement District, Chair of Keep Britain Tidy, Founder of Cloud Talking Aspirational Mentoring Company

"I have known Karl for many years, and have had the pleasure of observing him develop and advance the field of corporate governance. In particular, his concepts of compliance and performance drivers give a complete model for directing and controlling an organisation.

This book, entitled *The Effective Board Member*, based on this governance, is a 'must read' for anyone who aspires to being on a board, and for those who are already on a board but wish to know more about being an effective member of a board.

The book contains many illuminating insights into 'bad board behaviour, which we all can learn from when considering our own and others' behaviour on boards. Karl has produced a masterpiece for anyone interested in implementing best practice corporate governance and developing effective boards, and we will definitely be using this book to assist teaching and learning here at the PwC Academy in the Middle East.

Chris Cain, Director at PwC

"Karl can always be relied upon to share leading-edge information about good governance, and he does so with an enthusiasm that is infectious and entertaining. I am grateful to him for the support and guidance he continues to offer me and my trustees – he helps us all to be ever more effective in our work and the services we offer to others."

Brian Carr, Chief Executive of BVSC (The Centre for Voluntary Action) and author of *How To Find Your Vital Vocation*

"Governance is often a misunderstood concept and a word that generates a lot of emotions, at times including anxiety and fear.
In my experience it is about getting the balance right between applying the appropriate regulations while still harnessing the creativity of your employees. The Governor, through his excellent EBM Programme, demystifies governance, brings it down to a personal level and explains it in the context of your overall leadership skills and NED responsibilities.

The programme was a great refresher for me; I wish I had done it before my first NED role and I would certainly recommend it to potential NED's, but also, very importantly, to directors of companies that are growing rapidly as governance needs to help power growth not hinder it."

Geoff Cousins, former Managing Director, Jaguar

"Karl has developed an understanding of corporate governance and a method of teaching it that I find to be exceptional, including his simple to remember acronyms."

Nigel Cumberland, a founder of the Silk Road Partnership

"I have known Karl and his work for over 15 years, and have been privileged to work alongside Karl for the past three years at Midland Heart. Karl breathes life into a subject that is central to any well-run organisation in the private, public or third sectors – governance. Put simply, it is about making sure that an organisation has a clear purpose and is run well, for the benefit of its customers and employees. Through his work, Karl makes sure that people from any background wanting to help run a business live up to those values."

John Edwards CBE, Chair of Midland Heart

"Leadership and corporate governance have never been more important than in today's business world, and Karl George is the consummate expert. He has over 20 years' experience as a thought leader and nationally renowned consultant in governance, including accountancy, business and strategic development. Working across the private, public and third sector, he delivers exceptional services in this field. There are many people out there who have much to offer most businesses so this work by Karl is destined to become a by-word for awarding yourself an EBM – The Effective Board Member."

Paul Faulkner, Chief Executive at Greater Birmingham Chambers of Commerce

"For a director of football, which is a role that I aspired to gain, I thought the programme was just about context, but it taught me about the way the boardroom is supposed to operate, and gave me great insight and advantage.

I didn't know what to expect, but Karl's explanation of what we were going do, how we were going to do it and the work we had to do leading up to completion of the programme has been very insightful.

Completion of the programme was influential in securing my role as the Director of Football at Queens Park Rangers Football Club and has helped me to contribute effectively in the boardroom."

Les Ferdinand MBE, Director of Football at Queens Park Rangers (QPR) Football Club

"The PwC Effective Board Member Programme is a course that I really enjoyed. The amount of depth and information that I got about running a public listed company has been outstanding. This will definitely allow me to run the organisation, be an effective board member and be better than we're doing. It is a system of compliance and governance that will allow Aramex to become a better organisation."

Hussein Hachem, Chief Executive at Aramex

"This is an indispensable guide to good governance, drawing on Karl George's vast experience with a wide range of organisations. This guide is for the novice and the expert, no matter how inexperienced or experienced you are. It is insightful, relevant and challenging, and full of really useful examples and techniques. If you follow his recipes and advice, your organisation will be governed well. This should be standard issue with all governance packs."

Dr Christopher Handy OBE LLM, Accord Group Chief Executive, Professor of Governance Law at Birmingham City University

"Having had the opportunity to read an early draft of *The Effective Board Member*, I believe that this will be one of the most useful books on board behaviour within recent years. With well-researched and presented scenarios across the public, private and third sectors, *The Effective Board Member* is a 'how to' guide for the many personalities that make up the diverse, modern boardroom. Karl's friendly writing style makes this accessible for all levels of director or trustee, regardless of their experience or size of the organisation."

Dr Andy Hollyhead, Associate Professor at Birmingham City University, Trustee of Birmingham Museums and Art Gallery Development Trust

"I highly recommend this innovative, engaging and thoroughly relevant programme delivered by an inspirational trainer – Karl George MBE. The case studies and the interactive board game made for an engaging and practical learning experience. The knowledge, skills and the changed mindset gained have made me a much more effective board member and enhanced my leadership skills. The programme has been instrumental in helping me secure two recent board appointments in the public and private sectors."

Mushtaq Khan, Solicitor, former President of The Birmingham Law Society - EBM Programme Graduate

"Karl has unique expertise. Through his many years of experience serving on, as well as observing, boards he knows exactly what it takes to become a truly effective board member. He also has brilliant communication skills and if this book is half as engaging as his live training courses, you will learn a great deal and enjoy yourself on the journey. I have never, in all the training he has conducted for PwC clients across the Middle East over the last three years, heard him be asked a question for which he has not had an insightful and well-thought-out answer based on his encyclopaedic knowledge of the rules and principles of corporate governance as well as years of practising what he preaches. I commend Karl and his wisdom to you – I have no doubt that you will be a better director after reading this book."

Amanda Line, Partner at PwC

"What shines through this programme and book is Karl's experience and understanding. The real test of anything designed to support others' learning is the extent to which it is inclusive, not exclusive. The Effective Board Member Programme combines rigour with accessibility, widening access without in any way compromising content. If you want to be the best board member you can be, whoever you are, this is for you!"

Patricia McCabe, Managing Director of Central Consultancy and Training, and EBM Licensed Trainer

"The Effective Board Member Programmes give a clear and focused understanding of corporate governance, including the roles and responsibilities of becoming a NED. EBM doesn't just take a theoretical approach to becoming a NED, time is given to considering the appropriate personal skills required; e.g. challenging an executive team in a positive and constructive manner; engaging with customers and employees; and acting as a role model and champion for your company. EBM also provides an effective network supporting you in your journey to become an effective NED.

The programmes help you to develop the skills that enabled me to get the balance right between operating at a strategic level, without becoming operational, and understanding how to be reassured as a non-executive director, and therefore fulfilling my legal obligations.

It's easy to be put off becoming a NED; it can look and feel daunting. The EBM Programmes demystify the role in a clear and informative way, yet still manages to convey the importance and responsibilities of becoming a non-executive director."

Tracey O'Brien, NED
EBM Programme Graduate

"Governance, delivery and accountability are essential elements of organisational performance. Board members carry the ultimate responsibility to set the vision, oversee strategic direction, prioritise resource allocation and review performance. Karl George provides a unique blend of coaching and teaching to assist both individuals and top teams to shine. His emphasis is to identify their strongest personal and professional qualities, strengthening those while developing other areas of expertise, and guiding them to focus on their particular contributions and understanding, always valuing their own contributions and learning from others about theirs. Above all, his methods are about building self-confidence and trust, and this has proved very effective for those benefiting from his sessions."

Lord Herman Ouseley, Chairman of Kick It Out

“Serving on a board is an opportunity to help a company reach its full potential, create jobs and return a profit for the investors who have taken a risk. Karl George MBE draws upon a wealth of experience to transform the topic of governance from something that can be intimidating and dry to something that maximises the opportunity in a powerful and compelling way. Karl gives an approach to governance that isn’t about slowing down and avoiding risk; he helps boards to make better decisions, in line with their values, faster.”

Daniel Priestley, co-founder of Dent Global, author of four best-selling books on entrepreneurship

“I joined the EBM Programme with limited knowledge and a whole heap of unanswered questions, including if I was I really suitable for the role of a NED.

The interactive EBM Programme made learning a complex subject easy and engaging. The EBM Programme provided clarity around the role of a NED and increased my knowledge far beyond what I thought achievable in such a short space of time.

The programme helped me realise my potential and appreciate the value of my diverse background, building both my skills and my confidence. I have since moved on to gain a second NED position, this time as an independent NED, appointed to the board based on my skills and knowledge. The EBM Programme is a must for anyone involved in board membership or considering it in the future.”

Deborah Smyth, NED - EBM Programme Graduate

"It is generous that Karl George has written up his experience of effective boards and the behaviour which underpins them.

His insight, gathered over the last 20 years, is eminently practical, varied and deeply relevant... His latest work demystifies an obscure art. For sure, there will be something for everyone to learn and enjoy."

Andy Street, West Midlands Mayor, former Managing Director of John Lewis

"The quality of any educational course should be judged by its leader, its students and the on going demand. The EBM courses under the leadership of Karl George MBE; his distinctive, innovative style that he brings to his classes; the quality of his students; the excellent assessments; and future demand meet all of these requirements! This is exactly why the PFA has been fully supportive of these courses since we were first approached four years ago, as 'good governance' in all its aspects, not least inclusion, is a prerequisite for any successful organisation."

Gordon Taylor OBE, Chief Executive at the Professional Footballers' Association (PFA)

"We are very proud to be working in association with EBM in delivering their content jointly with PwC's content and thoroughly enjoy the delivery style and quality of teaching from Karl George."

Bruce Scott, Partner at PwC, Jamaica

"In the time that I have known Karl, following an introduction to him by a mutual friend, I have found him to be extremely professional, knowledgeable and credible amongst his peers, demonstrating a wealth of experience that proves invaluable to his EBM delegates.

He has a unique ability to create a 'safe haven' for delegates to open up, and share their inner most thoughts and ambitions. The tools and techniques the programme offers are practical, supported by easy-to-follow workbooks, and delivered [by Karl] in a warm, engaging, searching and participative manner, building the confidence of delegates as he goes!

Irrespective of background and aspiration, whether it is public/private sector, industry/commerce or the professions, the EBM Programme lends itself to appropriate learning and development."

Carmen Watson, Chair of Pertemps

"The Effective Board Member book is an excellent primer for existing and potential leaders in board governance. Edinburgh Napier University has developed a long and rewarding partnership with Karl George MBE, recognised in 2014, for a successful pilot of the Get on Board Programme as a co-curricular activity for university students, which won a Herald Higher Education Award for Enhancing Student Learning. Karl's teaching, methods and delivery are acclaimed by our students, and this book will be essential reading for future cohorts. Karl takes you on a journey in this book, acting as 'The Governor' and offering useful advice, as well as the attitudes and disposition to guide and shape you to be an a effective leader in board governance."

Dr Miles Weaver, Associate Professor in the International Centre for Management & Governance Research at Edinburgh Napier University Business School

"As Chairman of the West Midlands IoD, supporting directors is at the forefront of everything we do. If you are an executive director thinking about taking on a non-executive role or have lots of experience, this book will certainly help if you are at start of your NED career or are an experienced NED looking to seek further development. Written in a very clear and concise manner, it will be every NED's 'go to' book about being an effective board member."

Dr Jason Wouhra OBE, Chairman of the Institute of Directors (IoD) West Midlands, Director and Company Secretary of East End Foods PLC Birmingham

THE EFFECTIVE BOARD MEMBER

WHAT EVERY BOARD MEMBER SHOULD KNOW

KARL GEORGE MBE

tgf
BOOKS

Copyright

First published in Great Britain in 2017 by TGF Publishing
TGF Publishing Registered Office – MHA MacIntyre Hudson, Rutland House, 148 Edmund Street, Birmingham B3 2FD.

ISBN: 978-0-9544896-4-9

Edited by Elizabeth Muir

Illustrations and layout by David Hallangen www.hallangen.co.uk

Printed and bound in the UK by Impressions Print and Label
www.printandlabel.com

EU Ecolabel www.ecolabel.eu

FSC www.fsc.org FSC® C023367
The mark of responsible forestry

To the CEO and three executive directors at home

who sacrifice energy and time to support my dreams.

Foreword

Karl George's book is timely. Our country faces one of its greatest challenges since World War Two. Uncertainty reigns, but some things are clear. Never have wise heads and good governance been so badly needed. The future of our country and the welfare of our citizens will be determined by the quality, competence and foresight of public governance, at both local and national levels. The job of government is to determine, create, influence and encourage, and expect effective corporate governance both in the field and of business enterprises. Good corporate governance of our commercial, financial and production enterprises will be the key factor that influences the quality, scope and impact of our post-Brexit future. The term 'governance' is widely used and often misunderstood. Successful organisations, be they public or private, usually have transparent forms of governance, which largely encompass two basic elements.

The first is a recognition and understanding that all governance, public and corporate, has a human dimension in that the impact of governance on stakeholders is, or should be, central to all that they do.

I have been the headmaster of six schools over the last 30 years. Some of these schools had been condemned by Ofsted as inadequate. Every failing school I encountered suffered from poor governance and, consequently, poor leadership. I am currently a 'poacher turned gamekeeper' in that I am chair of two boards of governors.

In education, there is always a danger that governors may feel inadequate when it comes to challenging leadership decisions. A defensive head teacher can wrong-foot governors by turning a valid challenge into a vote of no confidence in his/her leadership. This is no less so where a powerful and defensive chief executive is concerned.

It is almost a given that governors of an organisation will fail if they are not clear about what their strategy is for the organisation. Key to that strategy must be clarity on the role of leadership. Part of the strategy must be establishing effective systems of accountability and performance management throughout the organisation. Governors must beware the temptation of acquiescing rather than demanding an explanation.

A hard truth is that governance is not an easy task. Governors are often appointed and left to find their own way. I can guarantee that this book will help any board member, whether they are described as a governor, trustee or non-executive director. Not only does it provide clarity about the roles and responsibilities of each governor in an organisation, it underpins the practice of governance with a sound theoretical framework.

Public governance is concerned with and answerable to its citizens. Corporate governance is concerned with and answerable to particular stakeholders, namely its employees, customers, supply chains, shareholders and investors.

The second and perhaps most important element of all governance is values. A board without a clear set of values will be sterile and doomed to become lost in its own barren environment.

These short paragraphs attempt to sum up what Karl George's book is about.

The key premise of the book is that good governance lies at the heart of all successful organisations and that good governance is about the transformation of institutional performance from its top to its tail. He is clear that poor governance can threaten the survival of enterprises, and that it can lead to chief executives and other board members facing public and legal censure for their failures. Poor governance has been cited as the root cause of the many very public and spectacular failures in recent times of banks, large financial institutions, NHS trusts and local authorities.

Karl founded the governance forum in Birmingham, UK. This organisation has gone from strength to strength, and has been effective in helping a wide range of organisations to improve, understand the role and perform its governance.

The book takes a board member on an individual journey through the snares, pitfalls and challenges of governance. It is a 'how to' book that educates and is thought provoking. Anybody interested in governance will find within its pages a mine of useful ideas and a super guide towards better decision-making in in the boardroom.

Sir Robert Dowling

President of the Association of Corporate Governance Practitioners (ACGP)

Contents

Preface

The Effective Board Member is a practical, no-nonsense guide to help you become a high-performing board director or charity trustee individually, resulting in more effective boards collectively.

After delivering the successful Effective Board Member (EBM) Programmes, to hundreds of individuals across the world from a number of sectors across the world, I decided it was time to consolidate and reinforce that training with this book, which is designed to support people who want to contribute to the leadership of an organisation by becoming board members, or any working in or interested in the field of board membership. The book will also help those that are already serving board members to become more effective by refreshing their knowledge, and providing them with new tools and ideas to enhance their skills and abilities.

In my own professional journey, I achieved qualifications in record time thanks to my use of accelerated learning techniques, mind-mapping, speed reading and other memory systems. I have incorporated all of those elements into the EBM Programmes and individuals report being able to recall technical content during and after the programmes, which is then showcased in the boardroom. I clearly then recommend that you book yourself on a EBM Programme if you have not yet completed one, as soon as you can, but, until then and as a means of refreshing your governance knowledge, you will find that the content in this book will help you apply those learning methods. One of the key techniques you will discover is how I use acronyms to help you recall information at the very moment you need it, whether that is during a board meeting, a one-to-one appraisal or at an interview for a board appointment. These acronyms will help ensure that core information is always at the forefront of your mind.

In addition to that, I am a firm believer that theory should always be applied to practice and the learning methods in this book enable you to do both. Once applied, the concepts of *The Effective Board Member* will teach you to make an important contribution to the governance of any organisation. The beauty of the principles outlined on these pages is that whether you are serving as a director of a private company, a trustee of a charity, a school governor or a non-executive director (NED) of a National Health Service (NHS) trust or other organisation, you will benefit from reading this book.

Some of you reading this will be senior leaders who already serve their organisation at a high level and are now ready to contribute to the board at that or another organisation. Some of you will have aspirations to do so. You will already have specific skills and experience in subjects such as finance, law, information technology (IT), public relations (PR) or human resources (HR), and this book will demonstrate how effective you can become in a directorship role with the right approach and application of key principles. *The Effective Board Member* will help ease that transition from making an executive to a non-executive contribution in any boardroom.

There will be others of you who are new to boards and being a board member, or have no board experience. Others may have some experience but no formal training in governance to support you in undertaking your role as a board member. Whatever your situation, this book will help you to become highly effective in your role.

Every organisation needs to be run by effective board members in order to maintain high standards of good governance, which is the key to the success of any organisation. The content will take you on a journey that covers the key attributes, disciplines, required knowledge and behaviours that every effective board member needs. Putting into practice the advice that follows will help each board member undertake their duties and responsibilities in the best possible way. As a result, the performance of the whole board will be raised and the business will be led to new heights of success.

The use of the word 'effective', in describing the type of board member that this book will help to illustrate, recognises that board members are leaders and not managers. They are strategic and not operational. Effectiveness is a discipline that can be taught, but it requires a particular perspective and the chapters that follow will help to reinforce that perspective.

In his book *The Effective Executive,* Peter F. Drucker states (1) that: "Intelligence, imagination and knowledge are essential resources, but only effectiveness converts them into results. By themselves, they only set limits to what can be attained."

My study of effective board members has revealed that they originate from a variety of backgrounds. They have different strengths and styles so diverse that trying to predict effectiveness can be a futile exercise. Effectiveness as a discipline, though, can be learned and effectiveness in the boardroom is no different.

In my experience, I have found that effective board members have all completed these five steps:

- They knew why they wanted to become a NED and this helped them to look for the right type of appointment in the right company where they could actively contribute their skills.
- They understand the role of a NED, both the statutory duties and the core principles. They understand their duties and the boundaries they must work within.
- They are specialists, experts or thought leaders in their core areas of expertise. They leveraged that expertise when it came to securing an appointment by demonstrating how they could contribute to a board.

- They have mastered the art of analysing, scrutinising and then influencing, and they make an impact in the boardroom in a positive and effective manner.
- They put all their knowledge and skills into practice and remain committed to making a positive contribution to business and society, and using the boardroom as a way to make an impact.

This book will take you through each of those five steps in detail, helping you to acknowledge and understand your core strengths, and adding to them some new skills, tools and insights. A key component of boardroom effectiveness is boardroom behaviour. Throughout this book, you will learn about aspects of board behaviour, both good and bad, and how to respectively apply and avoid them. The book takes you on a journey towards effectiveness, encompassing all of the aspects of gaining a board appointment, and so does not focus exclusively focus on behaviour; therefore, I recommend that to complement this you purchase the second book in the TGF Little Book Series – *Boards Behaving Badly* – for a more in-depth study.

Successful, values-led organisations will have a positive impact on business. We all have our part to play – let's do it one effective board member at a time!

The Governor

Introduction

Introducing the Effective Board Member (EBM) journey

The Governor will lead your journey through this book on becoming an effective board member.

He is an internationally established expert in corporate governance and the founder of The Effective Board Member Programmes (EBM), which, combined with his consultancy work, have helped thousands of people to become better leaders and board members, improving the capability and capacity of many private, public and third sector organisations as a result.

Under his direction, EBM has partnered with organisations including the Association of Corporate Governance Practitioners (ACGP), the Professional Footballers' Association (PFA), The Football Association (FA), Edinburgh Napier University, the Professional Cricketers' Association (PCA) and professional practices like PricewaterhouseCoopers (PwC) where the programmes are delivered across the Middle East and in the Caribbean, and business advisors RSM UK. These partnerships have created outstanding programmes catering for the specific needs of women, young professionals, footballers, cricketers and other sports people, senior executives, and chief executive officers (CEOs).

With more than 25 years' experience in accountancy, business and corporate governance, The Governor also works as a visiting professor, and is an established author and speaker. He is passionate about community development, and sits on a number of local, national and international boards.

His vision is to strengthen and empower our economies by supporting organisations, businesses and individuals through leadership and governance solutions. Ever the leader and influencer, The Governor has established a number of initiatives over the last two decades, and received many awards and accolades including investiture as MBE in 2004.

To aid your learning, The Governor has split this book into five steps.

The first step examines why you would want to obtain a board appointment and how to assess the skills you could bring to the role. The second step examines your role as a non-executive including your duties and responsibilities. The third focuses on everything you need to know about seeking and securing a board appointment. Step four provides practical advice about carrying out your role once you are appointed and the final step encapsulates the thoughts of The Governor on a number of crucial issues related to governance that board members will encounter.

Helping The Governor to take you on this journey are four members of the TGF Zoo who will be on hand in every chapter of the book and who are also on their own journeys to becoming more effective board members. In total, there are 12 animals who live in the TGF Zoo who each live in a different zone of the zoo according to how their behaviour is categorised. The animals are placed in the applicable zone based on research and consultancy carried out by The Governor. These four zones are groupthink, conflict, operational and passive, each of which represents a type of negative boardroom behaviour. Unfortunately, it is not within the scope of this book to take you on the journey of all of the animals in the TGF Zoo, but you can learn more about them by completing an EBM Programme.

Focusing on the four animals whose story you will get to know in this book, you will see some of their negative behaviours and other character traits, which have been highlighted to help us understand board behaviour in action. These negative, dysfunctional behaviours are enacted in boardrooms across the public, private and voluntary sectors every day. Together with The Governor, they will explore different aspects of governance, including how their own dysfunctional behaviour can affect a boardroom with each chapter featuring creative learning strategies, including governance acronyms to help you retain and remember salient points, and assist The Governor and his friends to take you on this journey.

Dysfunctional Board Behaviours

All the members of a board have to buy in to a collective vision and have a shared game plan of how to achieve their objectives. If there are challenging characters on the board, it can be difficult for the organisation to fully benefit from the skills and expertise of individual board members.

Dr John Carver, author of several books on governance, says: "…boards are incompetent groups of competent individuals". This intimates that just because the individuals who sit on a board are competent it doesn't mean that the board, collectively, will be equally or more competent.

We need to strive for a situation where the board collectively has the potential to be smarter than its individual members – and this is achievable. It is when the personality traits and behaviours of individuals lead to conflict, fear, reluctance to challenge or take difficult decisions, or a perceived arrogance that we are always right that we have a problem.

We all have our own ways of dealing with conflict in relationships, but in the boardroom it is more difficult to use the tactics that may serve us well in our personal lives. A useful first step in dealing with difficult characters is to define and understand what type of individual you are dealing with, and then adapt your response accordingly.

As you read the chapters of this book, you will begin to recognise some of the shortcomings of our four characters from the TGF Zoo and opportunities will be presented to instruct you on how to avoid them. The characters you will meet in *The Effective Board Member* are as follows:

The **peacock**, who represents the board behaviour trait of **conflict**. In the boardroom, a peacock could be an experienced Financial Times Stock Exchange (FTSE) director who has a lot of non-executive experience. Most of us can display some narcissistic traits, but the peacocks among us take this further and continually seek attention, fame, fortune and power. Peacocks see themselves as special, and believe they deserve to be constantly admired and celebrated. They may exploit others to get what they want. When you are confronted by a peacock, it is helpful to recognise that, although he or she appears arrogant and impervious to criticism, underneath there is a very fragile sense of self, fear of failure, anxiety and shame. It is therefore important to acknowledge their positive contributions. If you need to challenge them or give negative feedback, try and include something positive in addition to what needs attention and change.

The **penguin** represents the board behaviour trait of **groupthink**. Penguins are friendly souls who need to be liked and can therefore be reluctant to challenge others. A young leader looking to take on a more substantial role after helping out with charities and student organisations could exhibit this type of behaviour. Penguins want everyone to get along and they fall prey to groupthink because they feel a pressure to agree and conform. Penguins have a tough time making decisions, and are always seeking approval and support. This type of dependent personality means penguins rarely move into leadership roles despite their skills. Make a Penguin feel empowered to get the best out of them. Start by introducing responsibilities that stretch them and acknowledge their success.

The **bee** represents a negative **operational** board behaviour trait characterised by obsessive compulsive behaviour. The busy bee is overly preoccupied with rules, orderliness, neatness and a need for perfection. They are usually controlling, intolerant and inflexible. This behaviour might be seen in an experienced board member who now wants to take on the role of chair or move on to a role with a national government body. Their lack of flexibility causes them to be preoccupied with lists and details, and as a result they can be inefficient and indecisive, leading to meetings dragging on for far longer than is necessary and becoming unproductive. The bee needs to be encouraged to understand that they do not need to be perfect in order to be successful. They need help to understand that it is not always realistic or practical to wait for the ideal set of conditions before reaching what they see as the perfect solution.

The **rabbit** represents the **passive** board behaviour trait. They are scared of taking decisions and averse to taking risks. This type of behaviour may be seen in a younger person with no board experience. They don't know where or how to start on their board journey, and need support and guidance to gain confidence and develop their skills. Rabbits usually fail to make a contribution to the strategic objectives of the board and the organisation it leads. Peacocks and bees often dominate these people. They will let other board members dictate the direction and activities. An important trait of the effective board member is the ability to monitor, scrutinise and challenge decisions and actions. Rabbits are too scared to carry out this part of the role and inefficiency is the only possible outcome.

Being an effective board member means you will be pushed outside your comfort zone from time to time, but we believe that the rewards of making a difference and seeing the organisation you are passionate about thrive and grow makes this one of the most worthwhile journeys you can ever take.

In this book you can expect to see discussions between the animals as they, and you, are directed by The Governor on the five steps to becoming an effective board member. There will be many learning and reflection points along the way, and, as a complement to the EBM Programmes, lots of acronyms to remind you of key points.

Now, let's make a start…

STEP 1

Chapter 1

Why become a board member?

Chapter One

Taking the first step – considering why you should become a board member

The smell of freshly brewed coffee wafted through the room as four delegates arrived for the first session of The Governor's Effective Board Member (EBM) Programme.

Peacock was annoyed and wasn't in a mood to disguise it: "This is a ridiculous waste of my time! I've served on boards for years. Any organisation would be lucky to have me. Then, at my annual appraisal, my chair tells me I have to complete this programme! It's ludicrous!"

Penguin beamed at Peacock and said: "That does sound strange. Why did your chair insist you came on the programme when you are clearly so experienced?"

Peacock snorted and said, with a heavy tone of sarcasm: "Apparently I have been rude to other board members. Frankly I don't see it. I don't want to be here. I don't need to be here – but if I don't complete this programme I could lose my board position, so they say."

Bee was busily shuffling printouts of emails confirming the programme details and wasn't paying too much attention to Peacock.

"What about you, Bee?" asked Peacock. "What brings you here?"

"Sorry?" said Bee, looking up with a distracted frown. "I was thinking about something else. What did you say? Why am I here? Well, I'm always keen to learn new skills and find out about things, so when my fellow board members and the staff at our organisation suggested I come along I was up for it. Knowledge is power. But I've got a lot to do. Excuse me I must check my emails."

The Bee's long-suffering fellow board members were actually very weary of Bee's constant flight from one activity to another without finishing anything, and lengthy speeches that rarely moved things forwards and just made meetings last twice as long as they should. They had heard about a footballer who had completed the EBM Programme and was now sitting on the board of a club in the English Premier League as a director of football. His experience in football combined with his newfound governance knowledge made him an important part of the strategic leadership at the club so they thought the programme could probably help Bee too.

Friendly Penguin glanced at frightened Rabbit in the corner and preening Peacock, and said with a smile: "Well, I just came along because Bee and I are great friends, and when I heard about it I thought it would be good fun, a chance to meet new people and maybe open doors for me. I'm not sure if I'll get much out of the programme, but I'm a people person so it's a great way to spend some time."

Rabbit looked worried: "I found the programme on the Internet. Do you think it's all right that I came along? I just worry so much that I don't know anything about governance. Do I have what it takes to be a board member? Am I doing it for the right reasons? I'm really not sure if I'm up to this."

There was a snort from Peacock who said curtly: "If you're even thinking that, then you are probably in the wrong place."

Bee sighed and looked sympathetically in Rabbit's direction for just a moment. "I'd like to help, but, while I sympathise Rabbit, it's not something we've got time for right now."

Penguin headed straight over to Rabbit, smiling broadly: "Don't worry. It's fine. Bee and Peacock have got lots of experience, so we're all in safe hands. They know what they are doing. It's all going to be fine. We'll all get along famously. Look! Here comes The Governor now. He'll tell you."

The Governor walked into the room and introduced himself. He knew a little bit about the background and personalities of the four delegates already. He told them: "You each bring different skills and experience to the table, and that includes you, Rabbit. You are new to this role but you have a passion for the organisation you've chosen to serve, but don't underestimate the qualities you have and the experience you have had working with charities and student bodies in the past. The journey to becoming an effective board member never ends as there's always something new to learn, new information or a new perspective."

Peacock looked surprised and said: "I appreciate that's true for our younger and less experienced members, but that obviously doesn't apply to me, Governor."

"It applies to all of us," said The Governor. "Complacency and arrogance can lead us into trouble very quickly. We must constantly be evaluating our performance and our behaviours to make sure we're delivering the best results possible for all our stakeholders. We can all learn from each other, but that doesn't mean we are always going to agree."

Looking at Penguin, The Governor continued: "We join a board to serve and make a positive difference. That means we need to scrutinise actions and decisions, and challenge them if we believe they are not in the best interests of those we represent."

Shifting his gaze to busy Bee, The Governor said: "We all have a lot to do, but we must make time to listen to each other. Really actively listen, and reflect, so that collectively we can make the best use of our time, and make decisions that are better and stronger than if we made them individually."

The first step to becoming an effective board member begins with understanding why we want to serve. It is important to review and understand what we all bring to a board. This will be a useful refresher for those already serving on boards and a helpful guide to those seeking their first appointment. Acronyms are a significant part of how we will retain information throughout this book and on the EBM Programmes, and there are six core acronyms that you'll learn. The first, the **6Cs** will be learned in this chapter so look out for it! Now, let's see what The Governor has to say.

The Governor speaks

There are a number of reasons why you may have considered becoming a board member. I am going to take you through the main reasons, and, at the same time, review what an effective board member, governor or charity trustee looks like through what I refer to as the **6Cs**.

If you want to make a positive difference in business, joining a board is a good step. I believe that to have a long-term impact you need to have some influence at the top of an organisation.

What to consider before applying to serve on a board

It is vital that you agree with the vision of the company or organisation that you will serve, and are passionate about its customers, beneficiaries or users. The statutory duty of a director is a fiduciary duty, i.e. you are trusted to promote the success of the company or organisation. This means that you are part of making decisions for the long term and for the benefit of all stakeholders, which includes customers, clients, funders and regulators.

An important part of serving on any board is your ability to fit in with the people already on the board. Meeting new people and networking with them can serve you all your life. You will learn from these new connections and potentially from the people they know too. You will probably have heard of the concept of 'six degrees of separation'. This is the idea that everyone in the world is six or fewer steps away from anyone else through a chain of connections. The idea was first put forward by Hungarian author and journalist Frigyes Karinthy in 1929 (2). Everyone you come into contact with through your board work can help sharpen your thoughts and bring out the best in you, as well as forging links between you, them and their networks.

The SERVE acronym sets out the reasons to join a board

A key aspect of sitting on a board is the opportunity to serve that board, and its company or organisation. The role of a non-executive director (NED) is a challenging but ultimately rewarding one. It demands integrity and high ethical standards. NEDs bring valuable life and business experience to boards.

With this in mind I created the **SERVE** acronym, which will help you remember the key reasons why you might want to serve on a board, or as a governor or charity trustee.

S – Skills: As a board member you have to look at things from a different perspective and will acquire new skills in the process. If you have a functional skill, such as financial or legal experience, you will gain broader knowledge in many new aspects of leading and running the organisation you serve as a board member. Skills you will acquire could include raising funds via the capital markets, the latest risk assessment techniques, or new thinking on cyber security and technology. Board members will also learn negotiating and influencing skills, the ability to gather and interpret data, and propose solutions and recommendations.

E – Expertise: Each board member will have a specific skill or skills, and a unique background. Joining a board allows you to share your unique insights and professional skills with the other members. You have the opportunity to become the board champion in areas you are particularly interested in or where your skills lie. By helping newer and less experienced board members you will be supporting the next generation of leaders and encouraging others to become NEDs. In the Bible there is a phrase (3): "…as iron sharpens iron, so one person sharpens another" (Proverbs 27:17). This is certainly true of being an effective board member. By coming into contact with other board members with different expertise, you will find you sharpen each other's ideas, thoughts and abilities.

R – Remuneration: Most roles in the private sector and with larger voluntary organisations will pay you for your time. The one exception is charities, which only remunerate trustees and board members for expenses incurred in the course of their duties.

V – Value: Being a board member enables you to have a strategic impact on helping the organisation to achieve its objectives. It's a golden opportunity to give back to the community and support causes that are important to you. There are indirect benefits to you through the skills and experience you will gain. The first step to securing a board member role where you can deliver and receive the most value is to do your research, and identify the type of appointment and the sector in which you want to work. Choose an organisation where you can bring about a positive change and make a valued contribution.

E – Experience: You get an opportunity to experience different areas of business and different sectors to the ones in which you are already a specialist. If you have worked as a senior team member in a large business, then sitting on the board of a smaller organisation will give you the opportunity to see new things from a different perspective. The experience of being a board member will make you a better leader.

How the 6Cs determine whether you are an effective board member

Good governance is essential to the successful operation of any company or organisation, whether it is in the private, public or voluntary sector, and it comes from the board of directors. Clearly, the more effective the individual board members are, the more effective governance as a whole will be.

A school governing body, for example, should be made up of individually and collectively competent members. Every governor should have a core set of competences such as finance, leadership, education and HR. There should also be specialists with particular skills, such as the law, so that together the governing body has all the skills and expertise needed to run the school. The same principles apply to trustees and NEDs of other companies and organisations.

If you are involved in the governance of organisations as a board member, governor or trustee, you can measure how effective you are against core attributes, which I describe as the **6Cs** of an effective board member.

Some board members will have these attributes in place, but others may need training and development to operate at the most effective level possible. These 6Cs are as follows:

Competence: Board members need core skills in finance, the law, governance, general commercial awareness and HR. A core principle of leadership is having a vision and motivating other people towards that vision.

Commitment: You can be competent, but if you don't read your board papers or understand what the organisation does, how will you challenge and scrutinise the business or organisation, and its activities? An effective board member makes time to attend training, understand the organisation or company in depth, attend a full induction, read board papers, and attend meetings and committees.

Contribution: You can only be effective if you are adding value to the organisation, project or initiative that you are working on. To do this you need to make useful contributions to discussions at board and committee meetings, at events organised on behalf of the organisation, and at away days. Having independent NEDs who have no other connection with the company strengthens boards. They can be objective and their thinking is often less constrained.

Comprehension: In order to contribute and lead effectively, you must understand the culture, history and the objectives of the organisation you serve, and be able to communicate all those elements effectively to all stakeholders.

Capability: There are many soft skills that an effective board member should have in addition to their core skills. Key soft skills include the ability to influence and negotiate, to communicate, to analyse, and to think strategically.

Code: The seven Nolan Principles first set out in 1995 by Lord Nolan identify a code of behaviour that is essential to being an effective board member. These principles are openness, objectivity, selflessness, honesty, leadership, integrity and accountability. In addition, I would highlight the need to be decisive and determined. We'll look again at these principles in Chapter Four.

To discover how you match up against the **6Cs**, visit this link to take a quick assessment: www.ebmbook.co.uk/6Cstest.

Final thoughts on being an effective board member

The animals had received their first lesson from The Governor and completed step one for becoming an effective board member.

They had been reminded that before you apply to serve on a board you should take some time to reflect on the reasons **why** you want to serve. You should ensure that you understand how your skills and experience can add value to the company or organisation's existing board, and be clear that you are motivated to make a difference.

This groundwork will ensure that when you join a board you are in a strong position to deliver on the **6Cs** of effective board members. In turn, the **6Cs** will ensure that you can add value to your board and also to the people that the organisation serves. Commit the **6Cs** to your memory, just as Rabbit and Penguin did. Peacock was still standing a little aloof from the rest and feeling that this was all beneath him. He felt he'd managed very well to date without knowing the **6Cs**, but it was this arrogance and failure to listen that was causing his fellow board members problems. Bee was still adjusting to the need to listen actively and focus on The Governor's words without thinking about 101 other things. Her heart was in the right place and, as the programme continued, The Governor was hopeful that she would settle into the rhythm of learning new tools and techniques. A copy of this book would also reinforce the messages and help her retain the **6Cs** information.

In the next chapter the animals will learn about what the law has to say about their duties and responsibilities as NEDs. The Governor has a unique way of explaining the complexities of corporate governance and the next chapter marks the start of step two, which helps you with everything you need to know about your role as a board member.

STEP 2
Chapters 2-5
What is your role?

Chapter Two

Responsibilities that all directors face that you should know about

Penguin was looking pleased and even Rabbit was looking slightly less nervous after their first session with The Governor. Penguin said with enthusiasm: "I think it's great to see how we can all contribute to the organisations we serve."

Bee buzzed in agreement: "Certainly. We've all got skills and experience we bring to the table and the **6Cs** really help us to see that clearly. I'm **committed** to working as hard as necessary to get the job done."

Peacock gave a proud ruffle of feathers and said: "I'm **competent**, clearly, with all my years of experience in governance, the law and so many other areas of corporate life. I also have a good knowledge of the culture and history of my organisation, so that's **comprehension** covered. It's all pretty obvious and I still don't understand why I'm here. I don't need to know all this after all I have achieved."

"Don't be shy, Rabbit," said Penguin, with a warm and friendly smile. "There's no doubt that you can make a really valuable **contribution** to board meetings if you develop your confidence. Any organisation would be lucky to have you because you're honest and you would stick to the **code** of behaviour that The Governor reminded us about – the seven Nolan Principles."

Rabbit nodded in agreement. More confidence would be a good thing and Rabbit's whiskers were twitching with a strong feeling that the EBM Programme was going to be the place to get it. He was looking forward to hearing more about the Nolan Principles as The Governor had promised. Bee buzzed in again: "I'm a stickler for rules and regulations so I'm all over the **code** too. What about you Penguin?"

"Well, I think I've always been able to get on with people and those softer skills add to my **capabilities**. The Governor said an effective board member has to be able to negotiate and communicate well."

The Governor addressed the group and said: "I agree that each of you has the potential to achieve all of the **6Cs**. We'll keep working together on how you can develop your knowledge and become the best possible board members."

Bee was already scanning the paperwork to find out what was coming up next. Before he found it, The Governor explained that the next step of the EBM Programme was all about fully understanding the role of a non-executive. "We're going to be looking at four areas: the duties and responsibilities of a board member; the role of a NED; how a NED should behave; and, finally, the traits of highly effective board members," he explained.

Penguin leaned back and said: "It can't be that difficult. Lots of people are undertaking roles as NEDs. I'm very relaxed about it. I don't think there's much to it."

Peacock said: "Well, I doubt that there's much The Governor can tell me. I learned all about the duties of board members 10 years ago and I'm sure nothing much has changed since then." Rabbit felt a little bit sick. Maybe he wasn't cut out to be a director after all. The mere thought of legal responsibilities and statutory duties was plain terrifying.

The key elements of the duties of a director can be summarised as acting with honesty and openness, taking all possible care, and acting independently in the best interests of the organisation you serve and all its stakeholders. But there's more to it than that. Let's see what The Governor says…

The Governor speaks

Board members of a company are its directors, and the articles of association will give the board of directors the rights and guidance to manage the company's affairs. The board normally does this by employing a managing director, and delegating any of their powers to him or her. This chapter will deal with the duties of a director, and, although full-time executive directors and part-time NEDs have different responsibilities in the company, they all share the same statutory duties. Under section 250 of The Companies Act 2006, the term 'director' is defined as "any person occupying the position of director, by whatever name called".

Historically, the duties of directors in the United Kingdom (UK) were set down by a series of legal cases before being included in the Companies Act 2006 (4). They are also enshrined in law in other countries where I have worked including the Middle East, the Caribbean and the United States (US).

These duties include the need for independence, the need to act objectively, the need to remain loyal to the original purpose of the company and the need to ensure the company is well managed. These are known as fiduciary duties. They reflect the duties that exist where there is a relationship of trust and confidence. Essentially, the shareholders are entrusting their financial investment to the hands of the directors.

Directors are also required by law to ensure confidence is maintained in the company and its finances, and the risk of fraud and mismanagement is reduced. In the UK a lot of these requirements exist within the Companies Act 2006, such as the duty to ensure that regular financial accounts and other statutory documents are filed, and the requirement to maintain appropriate accounting records so that directors can clearly see the company's financial position.

For legal and public policy reasons, directors also have non-fiduciary duties to the general public and, in particular, potential customers. These duties can include prohibiting certain types of marketing that may misrepresent the company's goods/services, or preventing misleading information being provided about financial or investment proposals involving either the company or third parties.

I have looked at international law and there are three key principles that are found in the legislation of most countries around the world when it comes to the duties of a director. These duties (which are explained later) are as follows:

1. A duty of trust, which means that a director must focus on what is best for the company they serve (see sections 171 & 172).

2. A duty of care, which means that a director must be mindful of their conduct, decisions and judgement (see sections 173 & 174).

3. A duty to exercise independence by avoiding conflicts of interest and maintaining their integrity (see sections 175 -177).

The UK was one of the first countries in the world to establish rules setting out how companies should be operated. Today, our system of company law and corporate governance provides the framework within which all business is conducted. Our primary source of company law in this country is the Companies Act 2006, which sets out how companies must be formed and run. It has 1,300 sections and the list of contents alone runs to 59 pages.

Directors appointed to the board in UK companies have seven key duties in law, set out in sections 171 to 177 of the Act (4).

The seven codified duties of directors

1. **S 171 To act within their powers**: The first director's duty, under section 171, is to follow the company's constitution, and abide by the terms of the company's memorandum and articles of association. Directors are required to only exercise their powers for the **proper purpose**. They cannot go beyond the reason for which they are given their powers. This stops directors doing such things as taking company assets to line their own pockets.

2. **S 172 To promote the success of the company**: Under section 172 directors must **promote the success of the company**. When the Act was going through Parliament on its way to becoming law, this phrase prompted a lot of discussion. It hinges on the idea that a director must act in the way he considers **in good faith**, and would be most likely to promote the success of the company as a whole. To help clarify this concept, the Act lists six things that directors should bear in mind when making decisions and taking actions:
    - The likely long-term consequences of any decision.
    - The interests of the company's employees.
    - The need to foster the company's business relationships with suppliers, customers and others.
    - The impact of the company's operations on the community and the environment.
    - The desirability of the company maintaining a reputation for high standards of business conduct.
    - The need to act fairly as between members of the company.

In their annual reports, companies must explain how they have complied with their duties to stakeholders and shareholders. So, you can see that directors have to bear the best interests of a lot of people in mind. To help remind you of who all those people are, I use the acronym **GTS MOLES**, which stands for **government**, **traders**, **suppliers**, **management**, **owners**, **lenders**, **employees** and **society**.

3. **S 173 To exercise independent judgement**: There is a duty under section 173, to exercise independent judgement, that directors should not be proxies of other people. In the collapse of the Mirror Group of companies, Robert Maxwell was deemed to have control over the directors. Stating that you were only following the direction of another is not a good defence in relation to the breach of a fiduciary duty. Although the act makes provision for certain contractual arrangements for the execution of duties, where, for example, the company has agreed to act in a particular way, the principle is that directors are to act independently of the control of any other person.

4. **S 174 To exercise reasonable care, skill and diligence**: The duty of care in section 174 applies to the decision-making process of a director having regard to the factors listed in section 172. Directors must display the care, skill and competence that is reasonable for somebody carrying out the functions of the office, and if a director has any special qualifications, then an even higher standard will be expected. However, under section 1157 courts may, if directors are negligent but found to be honest and ought to be excused, relieve directors from paying compensation. Cases under the Company Director Disqualification Act 1986, such as the

Barings Bank scandal, show that directors will also be liable for failing to adequately supervise employees or have effective risk management systems, as when the London directors ignored a warning report about the currency exchange business in Singapore. A rogue trader caused losses so massive that it brought the whole bank into insolvency.

5. **S 175 To avoid conflicts of interest**: Section 175 specifies that directors must avoid situations where they could have a direct or indirect business or financial interest that conflicts, or could conflict, with the interests of the company. This applies in particular to information they come across in their role as a director. It is immaterial whether the company could take advantage of the same information or opportunity, or not. This duty has been consistently reaffirmed since the economic crisis following the South Sea Bubble in 1719!

6. **S 176 Not to accept benefits from third parties**: The purpose of section 175, the no conflict rule, is to ensure that directors carry out their roles as if it was their own interests at stake. Beyond corporate opportunities, section 176 requires that directors do not accept benefits from third parties. The act goes on to further describe the illegal practice of the taking of bribes, which is defined in the Act as "a gift accepted by a fiduciary as an inducement to him to betray his trust".

7. **S 177 To declare interest in a proposed transaction or arrangement**: Under section 177, when directors are on both sides of a proposed contract, for example, where a person owns a business selling products to the company of which he is a director, it is a default requirement that they disclose the interest to the board so that disinterested directors may

approve the deal. Failure to disclose an interest is a criminal offence. Sometimes, depending on the company's articles of association, the approval of shareholders may be needed for some transactions with directors, perhaps depending on the size of the deal.

The international viewpoint

Let's take a quick look at the position in the US and the United Arab Emirates (UAE).

In the US, when a person accepts a seat on a board, they automatically assume certain duties to the company and its shareholders by law, but slightly different laws apply in different US states.

In the event of any company dispute going to court, the judge will look at whether directors have fulfilled their fiduciary duties.

Under the laws of many US states, directors have two fiduciary duties:

- **The duty of care**, which means they must take time to examine the facts and come to carefully considered, informed decisions. This may involve them challenging management and asking probing questions to unearth additional information. If necessary, they may need to seek external and independent expertise.
- **The duty of loyalty**, which means they must always put the interests of the company and shareholders ahead of their own interests. Directors must disclose any potential conflicts of interest and stay out of all discussions where they could personally benefit. Directors also have a duty to act in 'good faith', which means acting with honest intent and never taking unfair advantage of their position.

US directors gain valuable protection from the 'business judgement rule'. This assumes, in the absence of any evidence to the contrary, that directors have complied with their fiduciary duties. It means that the courts won't find directors liable for a decision made in good faith and with due care, even if the decision later turns out to be a poor one with harmful consequences for the company, and its shareholders and stakeholders. In some US states, directors owe fiduciary duties to a broader group, beyond the company and its shareholders, which could include employees, suppliers and the local community. In the case of an insolvent company, directors' fiduciary duties expand to include the creditors.

Turning to the UAE, one of its key legal provisions is set out in Article 111 of its Companies Law (5) and states that: "...the chairman and members of the board of directors shall be liable towards the company, the shareholders and third parties for all acts of fraud, abuse of power, violation of the law or the company's articles, in addition to mismanagement. Any provision to the contrary is void."

From this we can assume that the duties of directors in the UAE include the following:

- **A duty to act honestly** – as is the case in most countries.
- **A duty to act in accordance with the law and within the scope of the powers set out in the company's constitutional documents** – also found in most countries.
- **A duty not to abuse the powers of a director** – probably including a duty to not personally profit as a result of a directorship.
- **A duty to exercise a degree of care and judgement in the performance of a director's role.**
- **A duty to act in the best interests of the company and the shareholders.**

The duties of a trustee under the Charities Act

Trustees have the overall legal responsibility for a charity and are answerable for making sure it's doing what it was set up to do. They may be known by other titles, such as directors, board members, governors or committee members, but, whatever they are called, they are the people who lead the charity and decide how it is run.

You must be at least 16 to be a trustee of a charity that is a company or a charitable incorporated organisation (CIO), or at least 18 to be a trustee of any other charity (6). You must be appointed to your role in line with the procedures and any restrictions in the charity's governing document.

You cannot be a trustee if you are disqualified under the Charities Act, including if you:

- have an unspent conviction for an offence involving dishonesty or deception;
- are bankrupt or have entered into a formal arrangement with a creditor; or
- have been removed as a company director or charity trustee because of wrongdoing.

There are more restrictions for charities that help children or vulnerable people.

The main legal responsibilities of a trustee are:

1. **To ensure that your charity is doing what it was set up to do**: To do this you need to:
    - ensure that you understand the charity's purposes, as set out in its governing document;
    - plan what your charity will do, and what you want it to achieve;
    - be able to explain how all of the charity's activities are intended to further or support its purposes; and

- understand how the charity benefits the public by carrying out its purposes.

2. **Comply with your charity's governing document and the law**: Trustees must ensure that the charity complies with its governing document, with charity law requirements and any other laws that apply to the charity.

It is your responsibility to take reasonable steps to find out about the legal requirements; for example, by reading relevant guidance or taking appropriate advice when necessary. Registered charities must keep their details on the register up to date, and ensure they send the right financial and other information to the commission in their annual return or annual update.

3. **Act in your charity's best interests**: Echoing the duties of company directors, charity trustees must take decisions and act in a way that best enables the charity to carry out the purpose for which it was created. To do this, trustees need to make balanced and informed decisions, thinking about the long as well as the short term. This duty also includes ensuring that the trustees' duty to his or her charity does not conflict with other personal or business interests. Trustees must not receive any benefit from the charity unless it's properly authorised and is clearly in the charity's interests; this also includes anyone who is financially connected to the trustee, including a spouse or partner, a child, or a business partner.

4. **Manage your charity's resources responsibly**: Trustees must always act responsibly, reasonably and honestly. This involves ensuring that the charity's assets are only used to support or carry out its purposes, and that no inappropriate risks are taken with the charity's assets or reputation. The charity must not be over-committed, and any rules and restrictions on how funds are spent must be followed. Special care should be taken when borrowing or investing money. Trustees should put appropriate procedures and safeguards in place, and take reasonable steps to ensure that these are followed.

5. **Act with reasonable care and skill**: Trustees must make best use of their skills and experience, and give enough time, thought and energy to their role; for example, by preparing for, attending and actively participating in all trustees' meetings.

6. **Ensure your charity is accountable**: Trustees must comply with all statutory accounting and reporting requirements, and be able to demonstrate that their charity is complying with the law, is well run and effective.

Final thoughts on the duties of being a director

Make sure you are aware of both your fiduciary duties, which come out of the trust the shareholders are placing in you as a director to protect their interests and investments, and your non-fiduciary duties to other stakeholders, the general public and potential customers. Remember **GTS MOLES** – which stands for **government**, **traders**, **suppliers**, **management**, **owners**, **lenders**, **employees** and **society**. Consider the involvement of all these people to ensure that you carry out your duties in line with the law. This applies to charity trustees as well as directors of companies.

The Governor had covered the statutory duties, but Bee was keen to know all about the role of the board member. She was in a hurry, as ever, to rush on to more information.

Peacock was showing off again. "I knew all of that already," he said. "There's nothing you can tell me about the law." Rabbit was feeling very scared. He now understood the consequences of breaking the law as outlined in the Companies Act 2006 and was seriously worried about ensuring that any position that he secured would be within an organisation that understood it too. Penguin was just happy to be around people that she thought were really nice and keen to hear about the rest of step two. The Governor had told her that more information about the roles of non-executives was next, followed by behaviour in the boardroom. Like Bee, she was excited to learn more.

Chapter Three

Understanding and preparing for your role as a non-executive director (NED)

"I feel that I really understand the duties of a director after that last session," said Rabbit. "I'm still a bit scared though. There is a lot involved. It is starting to make sense now. I suppose I should be reassured to know that there are laws in place to ensure that directors behave honestly and can't abuse their position. But what if I get caught up in something and I can't control what other people are doing? Oh dear!"

Penguin nodded: "Yes, **GTS MOLES** is a good way to remember all the people that a director, or a charity trustee, has a duty to involve and consider." Bee recited the list again: "**Government**, **traders**, **suppliers**, **management**, **owners**, **lenders**, **employees** and **society**. I like a good list!" Bee buzzed in satisfaction.

The Governor was listening intently and reminded them of the three things they had learned about statutory duties:

1. The fiduciary duty to promote the success of the company.
2. The duty of care in carrying out a director's role with care, skill and diligence.
3. To avoid conflicts of interest.

"But I wonder if and how the role of a NED is different to an executive director?" asked Rabbit, ears twitching nervously. "Does anyone know?"

Peacock's eyes rolled up towards the ceiling: "Well, **yes**! Non-executive directors, or NEDs as we call them, are all very well and good – well, most of them are. I have taken on non-executive roles myself because I know I can bring a huge amount to the table. But, frankly, I think that in a lot of cases it's the **executive** directors who do the real work. They are the action people at the sharp end of running the company. People like me in fact! We are bound to be more important at the end of the day, and better equipped to set the strategy and drive companies and organisations forwards. I'm not convinced that all NEDs can make the contribution I can."

Bee buzzed: "I think you are wrong there, Peacock. NEDs need lots and lots of skills and experience. They can bring a new perspective to discussions precisely because their views **aren't** skewed by what's going on in day-to-day management. They have a very important role in setting the strategy."

"Let's all calm down and get along, please," said Penguin. "I'm sure you are both right, mostly."

Rabbit whispered to Penguin: "Now then, 'strategy', that's another word that worries me. I really don't understand what it means in the worlds of business, charities and not-for-profits. I remember studying the strategies of army commanders in history lectures, but boardrooms aren't battlegrounds are they? Please tell me they're not!"

"Don't worry, Rabbit," said Penguin. "I'm sure The Governor can sort all this out for you."

"Time for our second session on step two – all you need to know about your role as a non-executive," said The Governor. "Let's look specifically at the role of NEDs."

Any discussion around effective board behaviour or good governance should always include a close look at the role of the board in setting or contributing to strategy. This applies equally to the non-executive board member.

Let's see what The Governor says, firstly about the general issue of strategy before moving on to examine the role of NEDs. In this session you are going to encounter the next of The Governor's six key acronyms. Look out for **SPARSE**, an acronym that will ensure you always have the essential elements of the NED's role at the front of your mind.

The Governor speaks

The UK Corporate Governance Code (UKCGC) says that non-executives should constructively challenge and help develop proposals on strategy (7).

In my work in the Middle East, the most recently revised code, in 2017, was in Saudi Arabia. It reflects the other codes in the region in stating that one of the main functions of the board is to lay down strategies, including a comprehensive company strategy. Get the strategy wrong and the business is doomed to fail! So, what do we really mean by strategy, and how can we distinguish between good and bad strategies?

As far back as the 6th century BC, strategy was important in military science. At that time, General Sun said: "…all men can see how the battle is won by the tactics I use: what no man can see is the strategy whereby the victory is achieved." (8) Despite this, the application of strategy in the business world is a relatively recent phenomenon. It is difficult to find any real evidence of business strategy until the 1950s and 1960s.

In the modern corporate world, strategy is often viewed from the context of corporate strategy. The theories it offers don't always seem relevant for a one-site business, a non-governmental organisation (NGO) or a family-run business. However, the principles are exactly the same across all sectors, regardless of the size of the organisation.

The definition of strategy, which follows, includes phrases in brackets showing how the elements would have originally applied to military tactics. After a brief look at the history of some strategic thinkers, we will see how this initial view has evolved.

What is the definition of strategy?

Strategy can be defined as "How you organise your business (deploy your resources), to compete for the attention of customers in your target markets (achieve your objectives), faced by competitors and other external factors that present threats to your business (defeat the enemy)" (9).

If we look back to the 1950s and early 1960s, we see that business strategy was focused around the development of large, multi-product firms. The key question for these companies when they defined their strategy would have been 'How can we maximise the opportunities that the markets are demonstrating?'

Peter Drucker, author of *Concept of the Corporation*; Theodore Levitt, who wrote *Marketing Myopia;* and Alfred Chandler, author of *Strategy and Structure,* all write about successful organisations needing to centralise their processes and get their strategy right before determining their structure (10–12).

A shift came in the late 1960s and 1970s. Important figures such as Bruce Henderson and the Boston Consulting Group, Henry Mintzberg, and H. Igor Ansoff introduced more sophisticated and resource-based interpretations. These writers encouraged organisations to consider their strengths and capability, and **then** the potential market.

Dominating the subject area of business strategy since the 1980s and 1990s have been Michael Porter, Tom Peters, and Hamel and Prahalad. Current strategists, such as Jim Collins, who authored *Good to Great and the Social Sectors;* Nassim Nicholas Taleb, author of *The Black Swan*; and W. Chan Kim and Renee Mauborgne, who wrote *Blue Ocean Strategy*, highlight strategic thinking (13–15). They all advocate that stepping outside traditional markets to create new markets, anticipating the unexpected, and appreciating what makes a business survive and prosper over many generations are the elements of a successful business strategy.

Tools that can help you define and implement a strategy

Strategy, in essence, is very simple; its application is less straightforward.

Strategy in business and organisations is really about understanding where you want to go in the long term and knowing the best route to get there. In *Exploring Strategy*, by Johnson, Scholes and Whittington, strategy is defined as "the long-term direction of the organisation" (16). How, though, is long term defined? Is it five years, 10 years or even 100 years? When we say organisation do we mean the business unit, the group of companies or sometimes a department? The challenges are many: How do we determine where the end goal should be? How do we know which product or service to focus on? Should we go into a new market or capitalise on the one that we are already in? How does the political or social environment impact on our decisions? All these questions help to determine the strategy that should be adopted.

It doesn't matter if you are a large multinational or a smaller enterprise, you can use strategic tools and thinking to help you reach the answers to all those questions.

Developed by the Boston Consulting Group in the early 1970s, the Boston Matrix is a marketing tool used to analyse and manage a product portfolio. It helps businesses to identify which products or services need to be focused on and which ones to eliminate from their portfolio (17).

The Ansoff Matrix was developed by H. Igor Ansoff and first published in the Harvard Business Review in 1957 (18). This can help to determine the risk of entering new markets with new and existing products and services as opposed to staying within existing markets.

As we move on from preparing a SWOT (strengths, weaknesses, opportunities and threats) analysis and PESTEL (political, economic, social, technological, environmental and legal) assessment, we can use these matrices to make strategic choices, such as how do we use our strengths to take advantage of opportunities and how do we measure the likely impact of the factors identified in a PESTEL to decide what actions to take?

In considering these examples, strategy should not be confused with the tools and techniques. The tools and techniques outlined will help you to form a strategy, but should not become a hindrance or be confused with the implementation of strategy. Every organisation should be clear about its strengths, and seek to maximise the opportunities available by having a clear understanding of the competitive and wider environment in which it operates. The directors should use this information to determine the strategy, and then review and monitor it regularly.

When an organisation knows where it is headed and has a good understanding of where it is coming from, it can ensure that this vision is shared with the stakeholders. That will help it to plan the best route to get there. A clear strategy will mean that you can articulate your vision and your game plan for achieving the vision, often referred to as the mission. Three to six strategic objectives will give the long-term focus from which the annual business plan objectives can be derived. The board can then monitor progress.

How directors can balance the time spent on strategy

We are continually reminded that the board's role is strategic, but sometimes it is difficult to get the right balance at our regular board meetings, which must also involve scrutiny, monitoring and control.

One way of helping to maintain an appropriate focus is to review the agenda to see how much time is being spent on strategic matters and also ensure that board appraisals analyse performance against the corporate/strategic plan.

What is a non-executive director (NED)?

We have discussed strategy and identified that a key role of a non-executives is to be strategic. So what is a NED? It is a member of the board who is **not** a full-time member of the management of the company or organisation, and does not participate in its daily activities. An executive director, by contrast, is a full-time member of the executive team and, as such, **does** have responsibility around day-to-day management.

The previous chapter highlighted the duties of a director; i.e. the legal responsibilities of the position. The NED has the same responsibilities. In the boardroom, both executives and NEDs collectively direct the company's or organisation's activities.

The Higgs Review was a report chaired by Derek Higgs on corporate governance. It was commissioned by the UK government and published in early 2003 (19). It examines the role and effectiveness of NEDs on boards. With boards now having to consider more than traditional compliance, stewardship and strategic functions, the role of the NED is even more critical. Board members should be considering emergent strategy, generative governance and adaptive leadership in a terrain that is volatile, uncertain and complex. The role of a NED is both challenging and demanding.

A NED must have integrity and high ethical standards. Independent NEDs bring an essential element to the boardroom. One of their major contributions is the wider experience and fresh perspective that they may bring. Boards are further strengthened by having NEDs who have no other connection with the company. This means that they can be objective, something which those with closer connections find more difficult. A diverse board is undoubtedly better equipped to constructively challenge and help develop strategy.

Higgs writes that NEDs need to be sound in judgement and to have an inquiring mind. He states that they should "…question intelligently, debate constructively, challenge rigorously and decide dispassionately. And they should listen sensitively to the views of others inside and outside the board." (19)

The SPARSE acronym will remind you of a NED's role

Unsurprisingly, I have an acronym to remind you of the key elements of a NED's role. Please ensure that you commit this one to memory. The acronym is **SPARSE** and stands for the following:

S – Strategic: They help contribute and develop proposals on strategy.

P – People: They determine appropriate levels of remuneration, and have a primary role in appointing and removing executive directors.

A – Ambassadorial: They maintain dialogue with stakeholders.

R – Risk: They ensure that financial information is accurate and financial control systems and risk management are robust and defensible.

S – Scrutiny: They review the performance of management in meeting objectives.

E – Evaluation: They undertake formal and rigorous evaluation of their own performance and that of the board and committees.

Four of these areas – **strategic**, **people**, **risk** and **scrutiny** – were specifically identified in the Higgs Review and now feature in the UKCGC. I added **ambassadorial** and **evaluation**, which are both essential skills for NEDs, to create the acronym.

Final thoughts on the role of a non-executive board member

In addition to being **SPARSE**, a NED should keep the following aspects of their role at the front of their mind:

1. **Triangulating**: A NED is required to gather the information from a number of different and unrelated sources in the company, and then use them to gain an overall perspective.

2. **Being visionary**: A NED should take a step back from the detail, and bring independent and insightful considerations to discussions and debate.

3. **Monitoring**: A NED is required to contribute to the monitoring of the objectives of the organisation, including key performance indicators (KPIs), and its performance against the stated vision and mission.

4. **Questioning**: A NED should ask questions of the executive to clarify and to bring challenge in a way that promotes the achievement of successful outcomes.

5. **Interrogating**: A NED should seek to interrogate the information provided to them to ensure transparency, probity and risk implications.

6. **Influencing**: A NED should seek to positively influence decision-making processes that promote the long-term success of the company or organisation.

7. **Probing**: A NED should ask probing questions that ensure the company achieves value for money, corporate integrity, meeting the requirements of regulatory bodies and following the law.

8. **Listening**: A NED should be a support mechanism for the executive, always listening to concerns raised and offering

solutions to improve outcomes. They should also listen to the views of stakeholders and integrate these into decision-making processes.

9. **Being Adaptive**: A NED should be able to move with the changing pace of an organisation and represent the wider interests of all stakeholders.

10. **Negotiating**: A NED should continually debate and discuss with fellow directors to find the best collective course of action, and should be able to negotiate to arrive at the best outcome for the company.

As the animals reflected on the acronym **SPARSE**, it was Bee who felt the most challenged by this session.

"It goes against the grain," she whispered to Rabbit. "Here I am being told to stay strategic and to scrutinise, but not get involved in the execution. That goes against all my instincts to roll my sleeves up and get stuck in when things need doing. I thought I was being helpful and making a real contribution with all my hard work. Could it be that I'd actually been interfering in things that shouldn't have been part of my role?"

Peacock was secretly in awe of The Governor. He knew he couldn't let it show or he might lose face in front of the three other animals. He would never have admitted it, but he was now really intrigued to find out what The Governor had to say about how a board member should behave, so let's not keep him waiting any longer. Let's move straight on to the next session of step two.

Chapter Four

Standing up for what is right in undertaking your role

"We've looked at the duties and responsibilities of executive and non-executive directors, and I think now we're going to be looking more at **how** board members should behave," said Peacock. "This is good because I know a lot about this already. I've served for many years on the board of a FTSE company and been a NED too, you know."

Bee and Penguin glanced at each other. Perhaps they didn't hold Peacock in quite the high regard that the proud bird imagined? Meanwhile, Rabbit was hanging on to Peacock's every word.

"Oh yes!" said Peacock, "I don't believe in pandering to the executive team. I didn't get where I am today by being a pushover." "Let me tell you," continued Peacock, leaning closer to Rabbit, "It's our job to challenge the executive. The Governor has said so already. What that means, let me tell you, is that you have to keep them on their toes! Don't, whatever you do, start telling them they are doing a good job – even when they are! Praise makes people complacent. It's a slippery slope."

Penguin looked uncomfortable: "I'm not sure that 'treating people mean keeps them keen'. I don't think it gets the best out of them. It certainly wouldn't work on me. I know lots of people respond far better when they are treated fairly and the good work they do is recognised."

Bee buzzed in: "I've got lots and lots of data on this subject, actually. There is plenty of evidence to show that it's very important to ensure that people feel appreciated. Many people don't leave their jobs because of pay or job security. For many people it's because they don't feel appreciated."

Rabbit frowned. "I'm confused. I think I need to hear what The Governor thinks."

The Governor was happy to step in. He said: "Peacock is right to say that board members need to be able to challenge and scrutinise the executive team effectively. It is a key role. But, this challenge must be appropriate and shouldn't create a culture of 'us and them'."

The smile on Peacock's face began to slip slightly. It was beginning to matter to him what The Governor thought of him.

The Governor continued: "Bee is also right to say that people need to feel appreciated. Understanding how their individual performance contributes to the success of the organisation motivates employees, and they thrive when they are made to feel worthwhile.

"When some NEDs are trying to be effective, they sometimes get too operational. They can feel that their duty to ensure compliance justifies behaviour that can be very demotivating. Employees should not be directed in such a way that they feel undervalued. All this applies to the ways in which board members communicate and conduct themselves in the boardroom too. For the board to operate effectively, and for there to be strong lines of communication and good co-operation, it's important that each member behaves in an exemplary fashion.

"Monitoring, scrutiny and challenge doesn't mean there can't be praise as well.

"We're about to look in more detail at how board members should behave, but let's start with this quote by Tom Rath and Donald O.

Clifton from their book *How Full is your Bucket? Positive Strategies for Work and Life:* '…individuals who receive regular recognition and praise: increase their individual productivity, increase engagement among their colleagues [and] are more likely to stay with their organisation'." (20)

There are some clear guidelines that board members can follow to ensure they are conducting themselves effectively and appropriately, both in the boardroom and when they are representing their organisation elsewhere. As we continue our look at the role of a NED, which is step two of our five-step journey, we are going to focus on the behaviour that we should expect from board members.

The Governor is going to share with you the thoughts of Gordon Taylor OBE, Chief Executive of the Professional Footballers' Association (PFA), whom he interviewed on the subject of good governance and top tips for new NEDs. He's also going to teach you his next major acronym – **OOHLISA** –which will remind you of some of the standards board members should emanate. Let's get going…

The Governor speaks

In 1994, the UK government, led by Prime Minister John Major, set up the Committee on Standards in Public Life (21)('the Committee'). It was chaired by Lord Nolan and was tasked with making recommendations to improve standards of behaviour.

It followed concerns that some politicians were behaving unethically – for example, during the cash-for-questions scandal. The Committee's first report established seven principles of public life, which became widely known as the Nolan Principles.

The Committee's original remit was to examine concerns about the way that all holders of public office were conducting themselves. This included looking into financial and commercial activities.

The term 'public office' is defined to include ministers, civil servants and advisors; Members of Parliament (MPs) and UK Members of the European Parliament (MEPs); members and senior officers of all non-departmental public bodies, and of National Health Service (NHS) bodies; non-ministerial office holders; members and other senior officers of other bodies discharging publicly-funded functions; and elected members and senior officers of local authorities.

In November 1997, Tony Blair extended the Committee's terms of reference: "To review issues in relation to the funding of political parties and to make recommendations as to any changes in present arrangements" (22).

In 2013, there were two revisions to the Committee's terms of reference:

1. "...in future the Committee should not inquire into matters relating to the devolved legislatures and governments except with the agreement of those bodies".
2. "...the Committee's remit to examine standards of conduct of all holders of public office [encompasses] all those involved in the delivery of public services, not solely those appointed or elected to public office".

Over the years, there have been some tweaks to the original seven principles of public life.

The 2015 wording (21) is as follows:

1. **Selflessness**: Holders of public office should act solely in terms of the public interest.
2. **Integrity**: Holders of public office must avoid placing themselves under any obligation to people or organisations that might try

inappropriately to influence them in their work. They should not act or take decisions to gain financial or other material benefits for themselves, their family or their friends. They must declare and resolve any interests and relationships.

3. **Objectivity**: Holders of public office must act and take decisions impartially, fairly and on merit, using the best evidence and without discrimination or bias.
4. **Accountability**: Holders of public office are accountable to the public for their decisions and actions, and must submit themselves to the scrutiny necessary to ensure this.
5. **Openness**: Holders of public office should act and take decisions in an open and transparent manner. Information should not be withheld from the public unless there are clear and lawful reasons for so doing.
6. **Honesty**: Holders of public office should be truthful.
7. **Leadership**: Holders of public office should exhibit these principles in their own behaviour. They should actively promote and robustly support the principles, and be willing to challenge poor behaviour wherever it occurs.

The acronym OOHLISA will remind you of the Nolan Principles

A valuable memory tip to remember the seven principles of public life is to rearrange them in to the order where the first letter of each value spells out **OOHLISA**:

O – Openness

O – Objectivity

H – Honesty

L – Leadership

I – Integrity

S – Selflessness

A – Accountability

The fact that the seven principles have survived and are still in wide use today, indicates their importance. Back in 1994 it was quite revolutionary to have such a strong focus on behaviour and culture instead of process. However, if board members follow the seven principles in everything they do, a side effect is bound to be a corresponding improvement in compliance and process.

How does an effective board member behave?

Moving on from the Nolan Principles, which shape your general conduct and standards of behaviour, let's look at boardroom behaviour.

Board members are busy people, but that's no excuse for rude and thoughtless behaviour. If you are to maintain high standards and behave in line with the seven principles, then you need to focus entirely on the business in hand at meetings.

Let's look in detail at the things you should be doing before, during and after board meetings if you are to be an effective board member.

- You must keep the information that you receive confidential; only sharing it with fellow board members and recognising your fiduciary duty.
- Make sure you read the agenda and any supporting papers ahead of the meeting. Papers should always be circulated in a timely manner – usually at least five working days before the meeting. Then, you should prepare questions that you will raise at the appropriate time, and think of ideas and suggestions to resolve any problems that are flagged up in the papers.
- If there's anything that's unclear or ambiguous, ask for more information ahead of the meeting, or seek clarification from the secretary or the person who has written any reports. It's also your job to highlight any typographical or other errors as appropriate.

- If you can't attend any meeting, make sure that you send apologies to the secretary in advance.
- Ensure you attend meetings regularly. Arrive on time and give the meeting your undivided attention for its full duration. Don't multi-task. A board meeting is not the place to be reading and sending emails and texts – however busy you are.
- If people are joining the meeting via video conferencing, be aware of time delays when listening/responding.
- Be courteous to other attendees. Respect their views, even if you disagree, and allow them the opportunity to speak without interruption.
- If you absolutely must keep your mobile phone switched on during a meeting, in case of an emergency, make sure it is turned to silent or on vibrate, and excuse yourself from the meeting if you have to take an urgent call.
- Don't talk when others are talking. Avoid having a private conversations or passing notes during a meeting.
- Contribute across all areas of the agenda as part of a team-based approach.
- Direct all comments and discussion through the chair. If it's appropriate, attract the chair's attention when you want to contribute to a discussion, then wait until the chair indicates that you may speak. This will avoid interrupting another member.
- When invited to speak by the chair, do so clearly, concisely, and at a volume and pace that all attendees can comfortably hear.
- Avoid the use of jargon, technical terms and abbreviations that may not be familiar to other board members. In your contributions to discussions, make sure that you use plain, clear language, and don't assume that people with different backgrounds and experience to you have prior knowledge of your specialisms.
- Throughout the meeting, be respectful of the role of the chair in encouraging debate, summarising discussion and clarifying

decisions made.

- Be honest, open, constructive and professional in the way you communicate an opinion or information.
- Listen attentively and respectfully to others, and be tolerant of other points of view, making notes of any points you would like to raise when an opportunity to respond arises. Do not interrupt when others are speaking.
- Be sensitive to the support that people may need when they are challenging or being challenged.
- It is your role to challenge inappropriate behaviour and/or language used by other members, either at the time it happens, via the chair, or after the meeting if that is more appropriate.
- Treat everyone at the meeting fairly and consistently, even when you disagree with their point of view.
- Challenge and provide feedback constructively, and ensure that any challenges are proportionate and based on fact.
- Challenge the issue being discussed, not the personality of other individuals taking part in the discussion.
- Seek clarification or amplification when necessary.
- Share responsibility for the meeting's decisions. Even if a member is unhappy with a properly considered decision, members must support that decision.

Top tips from Gordon Taylor OBE

I am delighted to have carried out a series of Governor Interviews with leading figures in public life and business. You can find them all on the governance forum's (TGF's) YouTube channel (23). One of my interviewees was Gordon Taylor OBE, the chief executive of the English footballers' trade union, the PFA.

I asked him for his views on good and poor governance. He talked about the need for trust within organisations. He said: "It is crucial that the boards set the example from the top of the pyramid right down to the base. I'd say that's good governance. Bad governance is a lack of transparency, lack of accountability and lack of responsibility."

I also asked him for his top tip for new NEDs. He said: "I think for any new board members my top tip is to sit down and listen, see how the board conducts its business, and get an idea of each and every one of your fellow board members. Listen to what they have to say and formulate your own ideas so that when, for the first time, you are asked to speak, you speak with a knowledge of your board members and your own experience."

I feel this is excellent advice, which we can summarise as the importance of listening, understanding and then contributing.

Gordon Taylor OBE also advises: "Never settle for the status quo. Always look to be improving whatever business you are in. Always aim to leave it in a better place than when you joined."

Final thoughts on how board members should behave

In order for a board to be effective and high performing, there need to be high standards of behaviour from its members and good leadership.

The critical issue is how the board behaves as a group. The competence of members is important, but the way in which they carry out their duties is equally important. Until the culture is right, it will be difficult for the skills and expertise of individual board members to be fully used. For a more a focused analysis of board behaviour, I recommend you read *Boards Behaving Badly*, the second book from my TGF Little Book Series.

An effective board should not always be a comfortable place. Challenge and difficult discussions are an essential part of the role of a board member. It's impossible to be everyone's friend the whole time.

But challenge must be handled with professionalism, integrity, honesty and objectivity.

The Nolan Principles provide a good road map for effective board behaviour and it is hard to argue against the values listed in the **OOHLISA** acronym. Remember this one as it provides a great foundation for the way you should conduct yourself both inside and outside the boardroom.

Rabbit was feeling a little bit sick with nerves as he considered the prospect of one day being called upon to contribute at a board meeting. But he was beginning to believe that if he followed The Governor's advice, all would be well. He could believe that it would not always be a comfortable seat at that board table – but perhaps it was true that nothing really worthwhile is ever completely easy.

There was just one more session to go in step two. Rabbit had been reviewing his notes since The Governor had covered statutory duties at the start of step two. Yes, he was really starting to think that he understood the role ahead of him a lot better.

Bee was also pleased to see that the next lesson would describe an example of a governance framework and a code of conduct to which she could sign up. That was reassuring and would help her turn over a new leaf when it came to sticking to her role and responsibilities in future.

Chapter Five

Traits that highly effective board members display

"My goodness!" said Penguin, "We're learning a lot about the duties of directors and NEDs, and how effective board members should behave. This is great. I really liked the **OOHLISA** acronym to remind us of the Nolan Principles. It's a great framework for how board members should behave."

"Yes," said Bee, flicking through more paperwork. "I agree that it's really important to read all your board papers ahead of the meeting and plan any questions you want to ask. I also take on board what The Governor said about not multi-tasking in meetings. I am so busy it can be tempting to look at my emails and do other jobs at the same time. I'll try harder in future to give 100% focus to the meeting and not get distracted."

"What's the last part of step two then?" asked Penguin.

The Governor said: "We're going to look at the traits of highly effective board members, and that's going to involve us looking at good corporate governance and…"

Peacock interrupted: "Easy! That's just about compliance. Tick the boxes and off you go. There's not a lot to it, when you've got the experience that I have."

Rabbit took a deep breath, summoned up some uncharacteristic courage from somewhere and said: "Actually, in fairness, I think there's a bit more to it than ticking boxes."

Peacock stared, slightly shocked by this comment, but Rabbit continued to speak in a rush: "I did read The Governor's *Little Book of Governance* before I joined this programme and I've got a copy here, look. He says, 'In order to maintain standards of good governance, every organisation should be run by effective board members.'" (24)

"Well done, Rabbit," said The Governor. "We are going to look at corporate governance and how it relies on highly effective board members who execute their duties well. You can follow best practice, and have 100% compliance with a code of governance, but that doesn't mean you will avoid all the pitfalls that can beset boards."

The Governor continued: "The UK Corporate Governance Code says that much more attention needs to be paid to the spirit of the code as well as the letter." (7)

"Boards need to take the time to consider how the organisations that they lead measure up to the strategic objectives and the outcomes that they are expected to achieve for the stakeholders."

Penguin asked: "So are you saying that good corporate governance is really part of a process that should be integrated across the organisation?"

"Yes," said The Governor. "It is not about ensuring there is a department or an officer to take care of governance. It should be ingrained in the systems and processes that the organisation undertakes, and it's not just for the board but also for everyone throughout all levels of the business.

"Reflecting on all we do is a crucial part of good governance as it helps us to learn from mistakes and develop best practice. It helps us to clearly see the difference between good and poor governance, and to help us in the training and development of existing and future board members.

"More importantly, being aware of how effective you are as a board member helps your board, as a whole, to avoid the scandals and failures that we have seen in the past across all sectors."

The Little Book of Governance was the first book in The Little Book Series created by The Governor and it does, as Rabbit said, highlight the fact that good governance relies on effective board members who execute their duties well.

In this final session in step two we are going to be introduced to another important acronym. Well, really it's three acronyms that go together to help us understand the TGF governance framework: **TIDY BITE** and **DOVE**. Be sure to look out for them. We'll also hear from a former managing director at Jaguar, Geoff Cousins.

Let's hear more of what The Governor has to say about the seven traits of highly effective board members.

The Governor speaks

Following a code of governance alone will not ensure your board is highly effective, but let's start by exploring what a code of governance is and how it helps.

A code of corporate governance is a set of principles and guidelines around best practice that companies are encouraged to follow. The format, content and principles of UK codes, and many international codes, today have been heavily influenced by the 1992 Cadbury Report (25). A committee chaired by Sir Adrian Cadbury produced this report which was, in part, a response to corporate scandals linked to failures in corporate governance. The committee was formed after the Polly Peck scandal in 1991, and its remit expanded as a result of the Bank of Credit and Commerce International (BCCI) and Robert Maxwell scandals that followed.

What is corporate governance?

Definition 1: "The system by which companies are directed and controlled." (25)

Definition 2: "Corporate governance is therefore about what the board of a company does and how it sets the values of the company, and is to be distinguished from the day-to-day operational management of the company by full-time executives." (7)

As these definitions suggest, governance is about systems, boards and what they do. A more detailed look at various codes of governance will demonstrate that they identify three keys areas:

1. What does a good system of governance look like? What is an appropriate governance structure for the board and the committees? What are the rules and regulations that an organisation must adhere to?

2. What makes a competent board and how should it be composed? We should also consider recruitment, induction and training, and the impact to be made by having diversity in skills and experience.

3. Finally, what the board spends its time doing is critical – what it focuses its attention on and how, risk assessment, financial scrutiny and strategic input.

Once an organisation has adopted a code, it then commits to the principles outlined in the code. An external stakeholder can rest assured that best practice is being followed. If an organisation chooses not to follow a particular provision in a code, it doesn't necessarily mean that overall governance is flawed, but they will be required to explain why they have not applied the code in that area.

Basic principles of good governance

In examining the Cadbury Report further, we find three fundamental principles that are common to what we consider to be good governance in the UK:

1. The role of the CEO and chair should be separated.

2. Boards should have at least three non-executives.

3. Boards should have audit and remuneration committees.

This establishes the principle that organisations are led by boards and the board itself is led by a chair. The CEO is responsible for running the organisation. The role of the board should be strategic, but, by the engagement of sub-committees, an organisation can make use of individuals who do not have a conflict of interests when helping to monitor performance, assess risk and ensure the achievement of the longer-term objectives of a company.

Good governance principles are the same across all sectors. Whether your organisation is in the private, public or voluntary sector, good governance starts with the leadership, the systems and the processes that the leaders have at their disposal.

I developed a governance code to help organisations tackle the key areas of corporate governance. The summary version of this code can be remembered through the acronyms **TIDY**, **BITE** and **DOVE**, which cover, respectively, resources, competency and execution.

Resources - TIDY

1. The board must be effective in leading the organisation and have an appropriate constitutional framework with the essential functions recorded in its **terms of reference**.

2. **Information** provided to the board should be accurate and timely.

3. There should be a comprehensive, accessible list of essential governance **documentation**.

4. All board members (**you**) should be aware of their role.

Competency - BITE

5. The organisation should ensure that its board and committees are **balanced**.

6. Board members should adhere to a code of conduct, displaying **integrity** and high standards of probity.

7. Boards should ensure there is a robust, formal and rigorous process for appointment, induction and **training**.

8. The board should undertake a robust process for the **evaluation** of its own performance and that of each board member.

Execution - DOVE

9. The board should establish a sound **decision-making** framework and ensure that it identifies its appetite for risk.

10. The board should be accountable for the organisation and the executive, **observing**, challenging and scrutinising.

11. The board should monitor the performance of the organisation in line with the **vision**.

12. Board members should act as ambassadors for the organisation, **engaging** with its stakeholders.

Having a governance code reminds people of the key areas of governance, and can also provide them with a methodology for considering best practice and the key elements of a governance framework. This also highlights the importance of their individual commitment to the boards they serve, while endeavouring to promote the long-term success of the company or organisation. The value of having highly effective individuals on boards is that they demonstrate collective responsibility, which is crucial for effectiveness.

Seven traits of highly effective board members

So, what are the traits of highly effective board members?

1. Highly effective board members reflect on their contribution to the board at each meeting. If you didn't attend the last board meeting, or you attended but failed to read your board papers, is your contribution helping the board to advance? In fact, are you making a contribution at all? Ensuring board meetings take place in line with the terms of reference is a step on the road to good governance, but contribution will be the driving force behind productive and effective board meetings, which help achieve the vision and mission of the board, and safeguard against failures. Ensuring the board has all the relevant, reliable and required documentation to carry out their role is something an effective board member will aim to ensure. Remember the acronym **TIDY** to keep the resources you need front of mind:

   T – Terms of Reference

   I – Information

   D – Documentation

   Y – You

2. Highly effective board members reflect on their own development. Reflective practice is widely understood as the process of learning through and from experience with respect to gaining new insights of self and/or practice. By reflecting on their practice, effective board members can begin to examine their board behaviour, contribution and the business of the board to ensure they are effective. Remember the acronym **BITE** for the competencies a board requires:

   B – Balanced

   I – Integrity

T – Training

E – Evaluation

3. Highly effective board members challenge, stretch and guide the executive. An essential part of board behaviour includes appropriate and necessary challenges in order to ensure the transparency of board activity. However, in order to avoid board meetings descending into chaos, challenges should always remain professional. The acronym **DOVE** reminds us that every challenge should include these four elements:

   D – Decision-making

   O – Observation

   V – Vision

   E – Engagement

4. Highly effective board members bring different perspectives and insights by staying up to date with developments in their sector and across the general field of governance. Being aware of policy and regulatory developments will improve contribution to board and committee meetings, and to the overall governance of the board. Having a current perspective and insight also means encouraging the training, development and continuous professional development (CPD) of board members at all levels so that your board can remain at the forefront of current practice.
5. Highly effective board members remain independent. It is difficult for board members to remain independent when they have become stagnant. While commitment demonstrated by many years of service can be an asset to the board, showing that the board member believes in the vision of the organisation, it can also lead to independence and clear judgement being eroded. Succession planning and the development of a diverse pipeline of

talent will ensure greater independence, and maintain the integrity of the board's decision-making processes.

6. Highly effective board members are custodians of legacy. Effective board members take full stock of the values of the organisation and hold these values dear. They commit to the very heart of the organisation and believe in the vision, wanting to deliver this to the benefit of all stakeholders. Board members, who are custodians of the legacy, take the time to learn about the vision and mission of the organisation, which can then be applied to their professional expertise to execute the duties of the board efficiently.
7. Highly effective board members are risk-aware. The global, political and economic climate presents some real challenges for businesses and organisations around the world. Effective board members will be aware of how changes in budget, law or regulation could have an adverse impact on their organisation. They are also aware of any specific risks relating to their fiduciary duty, documentation, inadequate systems or processes, poor relationships among board members, or the lack of skills and experience on the board.

A personal code of conduct for highly effective board members

Creating your own personal code of conduct allows you to see how the seven traits above are applied on a daily basis in your role as a board member. The EBM Code of Conduct is offered here as an example:

1. I am committed to, and take a full and active role on the boards that I serve.
2. I will complete and keep a record of at least five hours of CPD per annum in relation to my board development.

3. I leverage my networks and actively promote the organisation to stakeholders.
4. I deal with all affairs fairly, efficiently, effectively and sensitively.
5. I remain strategic in my decision-making and contributions to the board.
6. I understand and support succession, renewal and the refreshing of the board to ensure we remain diverse, relevant and effective.
7. I respect and adhere to the principles of collective decision-making and responsibility.
8. I ensure confidentiality is maintained by myself and others to protect the interests of the organisation.
9. I promote the consideration of corporate social responsibility, ensuring the organisation contributes positively in its local environment.

Whether you adopt the EBM Code of Conduct or create your own, it is important to ensure good standards of scrutiny, probity and performance become the fabric of your board.

Geoff Cousins on balance and good governance

In one of my Governor Interviews, the former managing director at Jaguar, Geoff Cousins, reflected on good governance and many of his comments echo the traits we have examined in this session.

He told me: "Good governance is a company, individual or stakeholders that actually get the balance right. They get the balance between applying and complying with the rules and regulations, and the commercial imperatives they have, with the passion of their people and the sometimes different objectives of the stakeholders.

"They are generally people who want to do the right thing, and they come up with the appropriate levels of governance and processes that still allow them to take the creativity and entrepreneurship of their people, apply that to a product or service, and take it to the market.

"So, good governance is getting the right balance between the commercial imperatives, and the rules and regulations."

Final thoughts of highly effective board members

In summary, as you take the time to reflect on your current, present or future commitment to boards, take stock of the seven traits of highly effective board members, and think about how you and others on your board can apply these to ensure that 'governance is more than compliance!'

Keep the acronyms **TIDY**, **BITE** and **DOVE** close, and remember what they mean.

Each of the four animals had one takeaway from this session that seemed to apply directly to them.

For Rabbit it was the **execution** element of **BITE** in the governance framework. He realised that you could have great resources (e.g. documentation), structure and processes, and you could have a great mix of skills and competencies on the board, but good governance means good execution too. In other words, challenging and stretching the executive, and making decisions.

Bee was coming to realise that she needed to be more strategic and less hands-on, so she paid close attention to trait number five and the need to retain independence of thought.

Penguin was focusing on trait number seven, and how she was perhaps too laid-back and easy-going, which didn't fit well with the need to be risk-aware and stay on top of changes in the budget, law or regulation that might impact the company, but without over-reacting.

Peacock was now in a reflective mood as the group reached the end of step two. The EBM Code of Conduct that The Governor had created provided him with a lot of food for thought. Trait number five was really poignant – he had previously thought it was only his view that counted.

"Right," said The Governor, breaking into their thoughts. "Are you ready to find out how to get that ideal appointment, ace it at interview and raise your profile so that you are always in demand? Well, let's move on to step three, which comprises four sections that will teach you everything you need to know about getting your dream appointment."

STEP 3

Chapters 6-9

How to get
an appointment

Chapter Six

The three things you need to know about gaining an appointment

After putting in some hard work on understanding the behaviours of effective board members, the animals were taking a well-earned break.

"That was a great section on the role of NEDs," said Rabbit. "I'm really looking forward to the next section of our training, which is all about how we get an appointment."

Before The Governor arrived to explain what they'd be looking at, the animals had a chat about their experience of how board appointments are made.

As the most inexperienced member of the group, Rabbit, was keen to understand how appointments were advertised. "How did you find out about the first board role you secured?" he asked the others.

Peacock's eyes rolled to the ceiling: "Well, it was all down to the circles I moved in, connections I'd made. You scratch my back, you know. We all helped each other out and looked out for each other. The good roles certainly weren't always advertised historically – at least not so that you could find them unless you were in with the in-crowd!" Peacock laughed.

Bee buzzed disapprovingly: "Typical! That's the sort of thing I've been up against trying to get a role as chair. Not always the best way to make the best appointments, if you ask me."

"Sure you're not a bit jealous there?" asked Peacock. "Having good connections is a huge advantage."

"We all network," said Bee, "but there has to be a fair process to get the best people."

Penguin stepped in: "Whatever might have happened in the past, I'm sure that, these days, appointments are properly advertised. But they can get hundreds of applications from very good candidates."

Rabbit sighed: "That's what I feared. How can someone like me possibly compete?"

"Its hard work," agreed Bee, "but it can be done. Put in the hours and do lots of planning, and you'll succeed in the end, I'm sure."

The Governor arrived to lead the next session. "We've been looking at some good, bad and ugly board behaviours, now it's time to look at the good, the bad and the ugly of board appointments," he said. "This is going to be the first session in step three, which is all about getting an appointment. We will then go on to look at working on your profile, preparing for a NED interview, and, finally, some revision and top tips."

He continued: "It can seem like a minefield to those wanting to secure a first board appointment – and things haven't always been handled ideally in the past on all boards.

"Today, most organisations and companies are realising that, in order to thrive, they need a fair and transparent process to ensure that they appoint a diverse range of people who can work individually and collectively to meet and exceed the organisation's objectives. A good board also needs to challenge and inspire to achieve a secure and successful future."

Penguin piped up: "So are you saying that there's more of a level playing field these days because organisations are realising how important it is to have the best-performing board possible? That's good news!"

"Yes, it is good," said The Governor, "but we can't afford to forget the bad and the ugly too. They are still with us."

Rabbit sighed again: "Oh dear."

The Governor smiled: "Don't worry, Rabbit. There are ways to get to where you want to be. I promise."

Securing a paid or a public appointment on a board should never be a foregone conclusion. It can be a long and difficult journey, and there are plenty of obstacles to overcome.

Let's hear more of what The Governor has to say that will help you navigate your way to your next board position.

The Governor speaks

What do I mean by the good, the bad and the ugly of board appointments?

The 'good' comes from a growing recognition that good governance is likely to lead to having a high-performing board.

This means that organisations are now creating robust and professional recruitment campaigns that aim to attract applicants from different backgrounds and recruit particular skill sets to cultivate a good balance on the board. It's good news for everyone that the process of board appointments is becoming increasingly objective and skills focused.

However, I believe that there is still scope to adopt even more sophisticated recruitment practices, in many cases, to improve diversity. It is important for boards to consider skills, but it is also important to consider the background of those who join a board. We need well-balanced boards that reflect the make-up of our society. Any business, charity or public body needs to serve a wide cross-section of society as its customers, clients and stakeholders, so it is important that the board mirrors that society.

I welcome the changes in approach that have led to boards creating a formal process to determine the skills and attributes that its members need to possess. At last, this provides an open and more objective process for board appointments than the 'ugly' approach of being in the right network. I'll talk more about that shortly.

The 'bad' relates to the number of candidates that apply for each position. I know of many examples of NED positions that have attracted hundreds of applications from high calibre, competent and experienced board members. This means that to secure a position you will have to invest time to ensure you can prepare. You will need to demonstrate the qualities that you would bring to the organisation.

The application process itself is quite straightforward, as I will demonstrate later; however, it does require a certain amount of work and success is not guaranteed.

When a vacancy is advertised and attracts huge interest, you have to do something to ensure that you and your application form stand out. Shortly, I will describe in more detail the steps you need to take to secure a board appointment, but I'll stress for now that investing time in carrying out research, writing your CV and crafting a strong application will stand you in good stead when dealing with the 'bad' of fierce competition.

There are many so-called experts who offer advice about the best way to secure an appointment. Gaining experience on the board at a smaller organisation or charity may help when seeking to secure a public sector appointment. However, if you are looking for a private sector appointment, be advised that board experience in a smaller organisation, or a not-for-profit, may not be enough.

There is also that 'ugly' aspect of the small networks that still cast a shadow over the issue of some board appointments. So let's look at that.

In the 'ugly' world of securing a board appointment, some networks still carry too much influence. Sadly, there are still some positions that are filled within small, closed networks. In these cases, formal processes such as interviews and recruitment drives are missing, and the appointee usually comes from the same background and culture as those who already sit on the board in question.

Trying to infiltrate a closed network is almost impossible and securing an appointment can prove to be a futile task. Codes of best practice address this issue by recommending that all organisations have open and transparent recruitment processes. Things are getting better – but it's not a perfect world yet by any stretch of the imagination.

The Supporting Principle of Section B2 of the UKCGC (7) states that "The search for board candidates should be conducted, and appointments made, on merit, against objective criteria and with due regard for the benefits of diversity on the board, including gender."

Hopefully, as boards start to take notice of the business benefits of best practice, these remaining closed networks will begin to open up. In addition, I further recommend that, when recruiting to the board, attention is paid to diversity in relation to the composition of the board including age, gender, background, skills and ethnicity.

In summary, the 'ugly' of securing a board appointment is, if you don't fit a particular profile, statistics say you won't make it.

Three simple steps to getting a board appointment

If you are clear about what you have to offer to a board, then getting an appointment can be split into three simple steps:

Finding out where the opportunities are:

Conducting research to locate suitable board vacancies is an essential part of securing a board appointment. Some of the initial groundwork will include identifying the sector in which you would like to secure a board appointment.

If you are seeking your first appointment, I would recommend that you search for positions as a governing body member in a local school or academy, or a position at a local charity. If you have unpaid board experience and would like to progress to securing a paid board appointment in the UK, vacancies within housing associations or at an NHS trust may be a good place to start. If you have relevant senior-executive-level experience in the private sector, now might be the time to start contributing at a non-executive level in a similar business to where your experience lies.

There are several routes you can follow to find information about vacancies on boards. These include:

a) Job listings in national newspaper titles such as *The Guardian* or the *Sunday Times*.

b) Websites including:
   - **www.wig.co.uk**
   - **www.publicappointments.cabinetoffice.gov.uk**, which lists vacancies in public office that you can filter by department. Appointments listed on this site include the

following bodies and departments: Companies House; the Ministry of Justice; the Ministry of Defence; HM Treasury; the Foreign and Commonwealth Office; the Department for Work and Pensions; the Department for Environment, Food and Rural Affairs; the Department for Business, Innovation and Skills; and the Department for Culture, Media and Sport.

c) Member-based organisations, which publicise vacancies to their members. Many of these charge a membership fee.

d) Networking. I cannot stress enough the importance of networking. By this, I don't mean the cliques and small networks that I have criticised for limiting the opportunities to secure the best people to their boards. I am talking about networking in its broadest sense. Networking not only raises your personal profile but also helps you to meet new people from different backgrounds and sectors. This in turn means they can talk about your positive qualities to their own connections. In networking, it's not just the people you meet – it's also who those people know. Networking can be a real win-win in terms of you learning about board vacancies, and also for you to meet new people who you can invite to apply for a position on your own charity or company board.

PARTY – a networking acronym

There is a useful acronym I have created that will remind you how to get the most out of networking. It's called the **PARTY** principle of networking and it will stand you in good stead for any business networking you attend for any purpose.

P – **Plan**: Start with a plan of what you want to get out of the networking opportunity. Research the event and the people who will be there, if possible, and think how you can add value, and demonstrate that you are trustworthy and likeable, so that people will want to do business with you.

A – Attendance: If you don't get out there and attend events, you will never know who you missed the chance to meet and what opportunities might have been available. Pay attention and be focused when you attend a networking meeting. It's no use being there in body if your head is somewhere else. You will miss out if you're not mindful of other people in the room.

R – Room: Work the room and have something interesting to say. But remember that everyone loves a good listener, and you should be focused on building real rapport and relationships rather than doing a 'hard sell' on yourself, your ideas or your business. Ask questions and really listen to the answers.

T – Target: Make sure you get permission from people to stay in touch with them. Ask for their business card, and establish a way that you can remember how and where you met, and what you talked about. They will be impressed when you meet again, and you remember their name and other details.

Y – Yourself: It's your responsibility to continually work on your networking skills, which include your listening skills, and your ability to build productive and collaborative relationships with new connections. If you make yourself helpful and useful to others you will find that networking works for you.

Getting an interview

Investing time in completing the application form for a board appointment will make a huge difference when candidates are shortlisted.

Alongside this, I recommend that you spend time on refreshing your profile and CV, making them specifically relevant to the opportunity you are pursuing. Perhaps you might get professional help from a recruitment consultant. This is particularly recommended if you are applying for a paid appointment.

Once you have secured an interview, you should brush up on your interview techniques and ensure you know what being a board member is actually about! You will also need to ensure that you meet the criteria outlined in the vacancy. For example, although some skills are transferrable, and I would not deter you from stretching yourself when applying, it's unlikely an organisation will fill a vacancy that requires financial expertise with someone who has no experience in that field!

Demonstrating that you are fit for the role

Being a board member requires commitment, drive and passion. You also have a duty to promote the long-term success of the organisation you serve. As such, you must show dedication right from the outset. That will include giving your time and expertise to ensure that your contribution makes a difference to the work of the board.

As a result, you must ensure that you are competent to effectively undertake the board role to which you have been appointed.

Advice for the interview process

Before your interview, make sure that you understand what the role will involve in terms of time and duties. Some boards will require you to attend full board meetings and also take on responsibilities as a committee member. Many committee meetings are held outside of the main board meeting. Ensure you can commit to what is required.

For example, if you are applying for your first appointment at a school, contact the school to arrange a visit and tour the premises. If you are applying for a charity vacancy, attend one of its events in your local area. Do all you can to ensure you raise your profile and demonstrate your interest.

Our EBM Programmes equip you with the right level of knowledge and insight to be a competent board member. Completion of the programme also demonstrates to organisations that you have taken the time to invest in yourself in relation to your role as a board member.

For more information about the EBM Programmes, visit www.effectiveboardmember.co.uk.

On the day of the interview, all the traditional rules apply: arrive on time, dress appropriately, be professional, ask questions, etc. After the interview, deal with any follow-up requests for more information, references and checks in a timely manner.

Once you have secured the appointment, ensure that you take up any induction process offered by the organisation. If there isn't a formal induction process in place, ask for an orientation to the organisation, its work and its people.

Schedule time in your diary to familiarise yourself with board papers and ensure you declare any interests you have that may affect your ability to remain independent when decisions are made. A crucial aspect of being a board member is making sure that you undertake training that contributes to your effectiveness.

Final thoughts on the good, the bad and the ugly of board appointments

So, there you have it: a rough guide to securing a board appointment. It may seem a daunting world, but remember that organisations are changing their ways because the failures of the past have taught them that good governance by an effective, diverse and high-performing board is the best way to achieve success and reduce risks. This means that if you do your research on finding a board appointment where you can contribute and make a real difference, and put the time in to your application and interview planning, you have a higher chance of success.

Remember the **PARTY** acronym to get the most out of networking opportunities that can help you progress socially, professionally and in the area of securing board appointments. It's a useful guide for getting on with other people in business and in life.

Penguin was a bit of a party animal anyway, so she really took to the **PARTY** acronym: **plan**, **attendance**, **room**, **target** and **yourself**.

Rabbit was a bit shy, but he welcomed the advice that people are drawn to people who are good listeners and ask questions. He knew he could show interest in others, and eventually build up the confidence to work the room and promote himself by demonstrating the value he could offer to a board.

Peacock wasn't ready to admit it yet, but he was more and more pleased that he had been 'persuaded' to attend the EBM Programme. It was clear that there was advice that applied to him that would help him achieve his goals.

Bee could see that standing back and taking time to think strategically was going to help her achieve her ambition of becoming a chair of a board. Being busy was all well and good, but sometimes you couldn't see the wood for the trees. She welcomed the advice on where to seek new board appointments and how to network effectively. The Governor had signposted them to a couple of websites she wasn't familiar with, and she made a note to check them out as soon as possible.

All four of the animals were now keen to hear more about securing a non-executive appointment to a board and ready for the next session of step three, how to work on their profile.

Chapter Seven

Harnessing your potential, developing your brand and improving your influence

Penguin was whistling a little tune.

"What's that?" asked Rabbit. "It sounds familiar, but I can't quite place it."

Bee snorted: "That's because it has all the right notes – but not necessarily in the right order."

Penguin smiled: "It's the theme tune to the film *The Good, The Bad and The Ugly*. I shall always think of that now when I'm thinking about how people secure board appointments."

"Really?" Peacock looked sceptical. "If I were you I wouldn't go looking for any appointments to the boards of performing-arts organisations!"

Penguin broke off from the musical interlude and laughed.

"Seriously, though," said Rabbit, "I feel that I understand a lot more now about how board appointments are made. But I still feel that I need a lot more help with how I raise my profile so that I can be a serious contender when a board member vacancy comes up."

Penguin smiled: "You are making progress, Rabbit. Good for you. It's very nice to see your ambition coming out."

"Is The Governor going to help us get our CVs in good order?" asked Rabbit, looking across at Peacock.

"Getting a board appointment is about a lot more than just having a good CV," said Bee.

"Don't I need one, then?" asked Rabbit.

"Yes, you do," said Peacock. "But it's not quite the same as the CV that might have got you to where you are in your career. Err, remind me, where is that again?"

Rabbit blushed and looked to the ground.

"PEACOCK!" buzzed Bee sternly. "Try and remember what people have told you and let's treat each other with respect."

"I'm sure I meant no offence," said Peacock. "Apologies, Rabbit."

"The Governor's next session in step three is all about raising your profile," said Bee. "I'm sure we will all learn something."

Rabbit looked worried: "But if I don't have any real, proper board experience already, and I don't, how can I produce a CV that anyone will look at twice?"

The Governor walked to the front of the room. He said: "One of the things we are going to look at in the next session is how you can put across the skills you have that are needed on the board of the organisation you want to serve. Transferable skills and experience are vital.

"Those who make board appointments will want to see examples of how you have actually solved issues, made a difference, and carried out a role that equips you for the challenge and scrutiny that all board members need to perform. Be ready for a question at interview asking you when you have successfully challenged a situation or a decision to bring about positive change.

"But raising your profile is about far more than just handing over a great CV. You also need to become a 'person of influence' in order to obtain a board appointment, and also to make a difference to the board once you have joined it."

In the first session of step three we focused on where to find board appointments, and we looked at the good, the bad and the ugly of securing them. Now, The Governor is going to dig deeper with advice on getting your CV ready to apply for the appointment you have in your sights and how to raise your profile to increase your chances of being selected. He also has some valuable advice to share from successful entrepreneur and best-selling author Daniel Priestley. Let's listen to what they both have to say.

The Governor speaks

As I deliver programmes around the world, one of the questions I am asked most often by people is how they ensure that their CV is appropriate when they apply for board appointments and how it might differ from a CV they submit for an executive role.

Let's start there.

Getting your CV ready

Let's give some attention to the best way to tailor your CV to reflect your board experience, or the skills you have that are transferable to boards, when you are applying for a board appointment.

Creating a CV can be a minefield! My initial guidance on this subject would be to remember that a CV is a factual record. Don't fall into the trap of writing ambiguous content that's open to different interpretations. When you are putting a CV together for a specific board appointment, you must be sure that you emphasise your strategic capabilities.

Right at the top of your CV, immediately after listing your personal details, it is always helpful to include a summary section describing what you bring to a board.

It is important to pay attention to any specific skills or experience that the board is seeking. If the board is recruiting to fill gaps in areas such as legal, finance or HR, ensure that you detail the knowledge and experience you have in this area. Keep the focus on how you can fill the skills gap throughout the CV.

You should try to provide examples or achievements that demonstrate your experience rather than just listing your experience. Begin with the most recent examples, focusing on the past 10 years. Other significant roles, experience or major achievements, which you feel the recruiter would be interested in, can be highlighted later in the CV.

Once you are sure that you have adequately explored and reflected your relevant skills, you should outline any board experience that you may have. If you are just starting out and this is your first board appointment, you must ensure that your transferable skills are highlighted.

If you do have board experience, here is some of the information you will want to include:

1. Name of organisation.
2. Role held.
3. Duration of service.
4. Details of any committees roles.
5. Your accomplishments during your time on the board.
6. Any quantifiable data to give context.
7. Any other responsibilities within your role (e.g. were you the designated person for safeguarding when you were a school governor?).

To complete the CV, you can provide details of any awards, qualifications and accreditations. Highlight any relevant leadership skills and governance experience. You can finish with memberships of professional bodies, and any published work or articles you have authored.

Do bear in mind the basic requirements of those who are recruiting. To make their job easier, and give you the greatest chance of success, the following tips are useful:

- Keep your CV to a maximum of two sides of A4, or three sides if you are detailing relevant governance experience. You can include appendices to list speeches you have given and publications.
- Font size 12 is ideal, but no smaller than 10 point. It might be tempting to cram more words in by shrinking the font size, but this just makes your CV look cramped and is very difficult to read.
- The format of the document should be clean and clear.
- Don't assume everyone will understand acronyms and abbreviations you use: explain them.
- Proofread your finished CV with care. Get someone else to check it over for you too. It might sound obvious, but the spell check on your PC or laptop won't pick up every mistake – although it's a good place to start.

Your CV will need a different focus depending on whether the vacancy you are pursuing is in the private sector, education, housing, sport or the arts. What you write must be tailored to the position for which you are applying. One size does not fit all when it comes to applying for board appointments.

Creating a written personal profile

There are two meanings to the phrase 'personal profile'. The first concerns the written personal profile that you are usually asked to create in order to be showcased to recruiters for board positions.

This form of written personal profile usually covers three areas: your career, any previous board experience (including work as a school governor or charity trustee), and finally your achievements and community involvement if contributing in the not-for-profit sector. A profile in the private sector may include a section on relevant interests, articles and publications instead of or in addition to the section on community involvement.

A profile should be concise, getting straight to the heart of the facts that matter and not rambling. A maximum of 200 words, excluding the sub-headings, is the usual standard. It should be written in the third person and I have used three headings in this example to help to focus the content. You do not have to follow this format, but it is provided here for guidance. If you do follow this format, remember to remove the headings afterwards!

Karl George MBE

Career and Board Experience

Karl George is an accountant by profession, multi-award winning businessman, accomplished professional speaker, author and visiting professor who specialises in leadership and governance. He has chaired and served on a number of boards both in the private and voluntary sectors. Currently, Karl is a board member and chair of the governance committee at a large and complex public sector organisation. As an entrepreneur, he has launched and run many successful enterprises.

About My Achievements

Karl is the managing director of the governance forum (TGF), a group of specialist organisations working together to deliver exceptional standards in the whole area of governance. He is the creator of the TGF Governance Diagnostic Assessment that has been delivered to more than 100 organisations across all sectors and was endorsed by the late Sir Adrian Cadbury. He is now one of the country's leading speakers and business coaches in the fields of governance, leadership and strategy, and is also sought after internationally.

About My Community Involvement

Amongst his many achievements, Karl was the founding president of the first international chapter of 100 Black Men of America, voted in the Power 50's most influential people in the West Midlands, and was chosen as one of the 20 national role models by the Department for Communities and Local Government as part of the Reach campaign. He regularly gives back to the community through contributing in his role as a member of many boards, which are both local and national.

Building your personal profile

The second type of personal profile, which impacts heavily on the likelihood of you securing a board appointment, is the profile you have in public life.

Building a personal profile is about the image you show to the world. It's your personal brand and it can be the most powerful contribution to your own personal success. It also contributes massively to the success of the organisation you join. Your personal profile can help the board and its organisation to succeed, and achieve all their goals and objectives.

In the course of my work with TGF I have carried out a series of Governor Interviews, and one of the most relevant to the area of building a personal profile was with entrepreneur, author and speaker Daniel Priestley.

Daniel's entrepreneurial journey started when he was just 21. By the age of 25 he had built a multi-million-dollar, international, event, marketing and management business. He is also a successful international speaker and is currently the KPMG ambassador for enterprise.

In 2016 he was listed in the top 25 of the Smith & Williamson Power 100 (26), which singles out and celebrates the influencers who champion, and have the greatest impact on, other entrepreneurs. Daniel is the author of best-selling books *Key Person of Influence*, *Entrepreneur Revolution* and *Oversubscribed*.

It is his thoughts around how you become a key person of influence that are particularly relevant when you want to raise your profile ahead of securing the board appointment that is in your sights. They continue to be vital once you have taken up an appointment as they are crucial to the difference you can make as an effective board member. So, I want to focus on Daniel's advice next.

The five Ps of becoming a key person of influence

When I interviewed Daniel, I asked him what he believed were some of the most important things people can do, as a prospective board member, to raise their profile.

He gave me five Ps, which he describes as the five core competencies of becoming a person of influence. Here's a summary of what he told me:

1. **Pitch**: This is about your ability to **pitch** the vision of the business or organisation you join. It should be non-negotiable that every board member should be powerful when they are pitching that business in the marketplace. You don't know who the board members are going to bump into at conferences, or in their business or social lives, so we want to make sure that every single board member can powerfully pitch the vision, the mission and the values of the organisation, and where it is going. Pitching skills are very important.
2. **Published**: The second skill is about **published** content. We live in a world where even small companies can have a workforce spread across a wide geographical area. Publishing documents that allow people to get on the same page of the organisation and publishing documents that showcase what the organisation is doing to the wider marketplace is a really powerful strategy. You might create and publish reports, blogs, articles, even tweets. Of course, there is a right way and a wrong way to put your ideas and opinions out there, but publishing is a powerful strategy.
3. **Productisation**: The third thing that boards and key persons of influence need to be thinking about is **productisation**. Products and services are fast changing and fast evolving, regardless of what industry you are in. Even if you are in a traditional professional-services industry and it's very established, it's still going to be disrupted by new products. If you are in a new industry, the

products are going to change very rapidly, and all board members really have to be intimately connected to the products of the business, and how that could change and evolve over time. When Daniel talks about products he also means the very essence or the DNA, or the intellectual property of the organisation.

4. **Profile**: The ability to raise the **profile** of yourself and the organisation is another powerful core competency. If you are featured in magazines, featured in YouTube videos, featured as a speaker at a conference or featured in the media, these are all powerful for profile-building for individual board members, but also for the company or organisation they lead.
5. **Partnerships**: It is the responsibility of every high-performing board member to put together win-win **partnerships**. Daniel urges all board members to be constantly on the lookout for really great partnerships that they can introduce to their organisation. This is where the connections you have made, your business, and professional and community networks are a vital advantage.

Final thoughts on working on your profile

Your profile is vital to helping you secure a board appointment – but it remains important to the way you carry out your role once you have a seat on the board.

The networking that you have done, and continue to do, helps you to become a key person of influence. The profile and visibility you have in your sector, and in the community, stands you in good stead when it comes to getting onto a board.

Getting articles published online and in print, and securing positive media coverage will put you in the spotlight, and enable you to pitch and promote your organisation. Recruiters will see clearly the experience and abilities you would bring to the board. It is still important to produce a CV and a written personal profile summary, which are tailored to the role you want and the benefits you would bring to plug any skills gap.

Bee had paid close attention to the comment that it was essential to stress your strategic capabilities when you are preparing your CV for a board appointment. She realised that, in her quest to become a chair of a board, she needed to emphasise and demonstrate her ability to think and act strategically. Being a busy worker bee wasn't always the answer. Effective board members have to be strategic more than operational.

Rabbit liked the five Ps of becoming a person of influence. He could see how he could start building his personal profile online and in the real world. It would take some work, but he was up for it.

Penguin was naturally sociable, but was starting to realise that her friendly chitchat with everyone needed to have purpose and direction. She could see lots of opportunities to work with the media and on social media to spotlight her credentials and achievements. Maybe she had been sitting back a bit and being too relaxed in her approach?

Peacock liked the sound of Daniel Priestley. His achievements impressed Peacock, so he was prepared to listen and acknowledge the sense of what he said.

Now it was time to move on to interview preparation in the third session of step three.

Chapter Eight

Easy steps to ensure you secure that non-executive director (NED) interview

Bee was happy: "I'm loving this. We're really flying through step three on getting an appointment now!"

Penguin smiled and nodded: "It's certainly all falling into place nicely. We've learned how to find out where board appointments are advertised and heard how things are becoming fairer when you want to throw your hat into the ring."

Peacock said: "I have to agree that it's a good thing that companies and organisations, and their boards, have come to realise that performance is improved when boards are diverse, and members are appointed through a rigorous and transparent process that doesn't rely on the bad, old, 'you scratch my back, I scratch yours' mentality."

"Agreed," said the ever-smiling Penguin. "Then The Governor gave us that really clear advice on how we put together a CV and raise our profile to help us secure an appointment."

"Yes," said Bee. "And it's so important to remember that maintaining and building a profile is just as vital to the way you carry out your role as a board member once you have been appointed. It's a real win-win strategy."

The Governor had been listening from the back of the room and now walked forwards.

"I'm really proud of you," he said. "You are starting to use words that make me 'tingly'! Words like 'rigorous', 'transparent' and 'strategy' – it shows me that you're making great progress in understanding what makes an effective board member."

Rabbit looked up and sighed: "I hope you can settle my nerves on a subject that follows on from all that we've been talking about. I'm really worried about what will happen when I am fortunate enough to be offered an interview."

"I'm happy to do that," said The Governor. "This session will recap some of the ground that we have already covered, but I think it's important that we do so to consolidate the knowledge you have built up and ensure that you are well-equipped to succeed when you are ready for your first, or your next, board appointment.

"In this session I'm also going to share with you some insights from experienced non-executives to help you develop confidence as you prepare for future interviews."

It's an old adage – but true – that success depends on preparation. When you are working towards being appointed to the board of a company or organisation, you need to lay the right foundations.

Here, The Governor is going to recap on the steps that will help you secure an invitation to an interview before going on to look at what you need to do to prepare for the big day itself. The chapter concludes with top tips from three other experienced non-executives.

The Governor speaks

Let's start by looking at four steps that will help you increase your chances of securing an interview for a NED position.

Decide what sector you want to work in and the type of appointment you want

Do you want a paid appointment or are you willing to undertake a voluntary role? A voluntary role may tie in with a particular charitable cause that you feel strongly about. It's also a possible first step if you have not had any previous board experience.

If you are seeking a paid appointment, you will need to decide what level of remuneration you want to receive. Payment for NED roles can begin at a few thousand pounds per annum, moving up to more than £60,000 per annum for public appointments and well over £100,000 in the private sector. Payment will depend on experience and suitability for the advertised role – so take that into account when you are identifying possible roles. Be realistic about what you can bring to the role and what you will be able to achieve. Don't rule out advisory committees or government appointments when considering where to apply.

Where could your expertise make a measurable, positive difference? Do you have knowledge in housing, health, education or sport? Is your background in business, criminal justice, the public sector or the civil service? If you have multiple areas of expertise, you need to decide which area you want to focus on and how you can best apply your specialist skills.

Legal and financial skills are needed across all sectors, so if this is your area of special expertise, you will have more choice of roles you could apply for; however, you will be assessed on other characteristics, traits and abilities too. It is the overall contribution you can make that will be measured by recruiters. Be aware that any board member needs to have the ability to contribute on general areas such as finance too, even if that's not your specialist skill.

Think outside the box about the transferable skills and experience you have that organisations may require on their board.

Think about the areas of interest you have outside of work that may give you ideas for areas where you could contribute as a NED. A board appointment might provide you with a valuable opportunity to try something different. Please bear in mind that you will need to have the skills required by the board, but do explore chances to move outside of your sector.

Finding vacant board roles

We looked at aspects of where to search for appointments when we explored The Good, The Bad and The Ugly of Board Appointments in Chapter Six, but here's a timely reminder.

- Board appointments are advertised in job listings in the national press, such as *The Guardian* and *The Sunday Times*, in sector-specific publications such as *Inside Housing* and *Governance & Compliance Magazine,* and similar global publications.
- Websites that advertise board vacancies include www.wig.co.uk.
- Vacancies in public office are listed in www.publicappointments.cabinetoffice.gov.uk, where they can be filtered by department.
- Member-based organisations advertise relevant board member vacancies. For example, the Whitehall and Industry Group, nonexecutivedirectors.com, local chambers of commerce and womenonboards.net.
- Networking is important for finding out about vacant roles. In fact, I cannot stress enough how important it is to network, both formally and informally, to raise your profile, and build

relationships with people who can alert you to vacancies and may suggest you to boards that are recruiting. Meeting people from different backgrounds and sectors multiplies your chances of getting on the radar of people who can champion your cause.

Update your CV

As covered in the previous chapter, it's vital to tailor your CV to the specific position you are seeking. If you are completing an application form and don't need to enclose a CV, then ensure that you focus on relevant examples of your experience and achievements.

Don't just list what you have done but explain how you did it and what the outcomes were. This demonstrates to organisations that you have hands-on experience of particular issues rather than just knowledge of them. Collate case studies and examples of how you have made an impact, where you have challenged an executive or brought about change.

It sounds obvious, but do keep your CV up to date! Experience from the last 10 years is the best to include, but, where relevant, other notable experience and achievements can be listed as well.

Make applications!

You've got to be 'in it to win it', as they say. When it's time to put pen to paper – or fingers to keyboard – make sure that you allocate enough time to complete the application in the detail required. If you rush through without the right amount of thought and preparation, you could be ruining your chances of getting an interview. The delegates of my EBM Programmes who are successful in securing interviews are the ones who have a disciplined, regular and methodical approach to making applications.

You must set time aside to send in as many applications as necessary for the type of appointment you want. Some appointments in the voluntary sector may not get many applications, but others will get 50 to 100 applications.

Ensure you read the advert, role description and any other supporting information about the position thoroughly. When updating your CV, ensure you cover all the points detailed in these documents to demonstrate you meet the criteria. Keep your information and examples specific to the position on offer.

Preparing for your interview

You've done your homework, you've spent the required time compiling a relevant, focused CV and application form, and (drum roll) you've been offered an interview! Congratulations! So what happens next? All the traditional advice about attending an interview, of which you will be well aware, remains valid.

When you applied, you tailored your CV to demonstrate how your skills and experience match up to the needs of the organisation, but when you hear that you have got an interview it is a good time to check through it again in case there are any gaps you will want to explain in your interview, or details you want to bring out and expand upon. You will have researched the organisation and its needs, but check again now for any recent developments in latest news, and reports online and in print.

Prepare a list of the questions you are likely to be asked. Rehearse your answers thoroughly and practice a succinct, verbal summary of any case studies and examples of challenges you have overcome that will be helpful in demonstrating why you are a perfect fit for this role. Respect the time of the interview panel and only prepare what you have been asked to deliver. Few interviews will have time for you to present with visual aids.

On the day, don't forget the basics in terms of making sure you have left enough travelling time to get to the interview venue and that you take with you any board information you have been sent. Your research will have helped you to understand if the board is recruiting to fill a specific gap in the skills, knowledge and experience of its NEDs.

Make sure you have looked at the organisation's website, recent press releases and media coverage, and researched current members of the board using websites such as LinkedIn to understand what they are looking for. Perhaps they need to bring in someone with experience in a certain sector or from a particular professional background?

Is the organisation facing a new challenge or a change in direction, which signals a need to strengthen its expertise in certain areas? Is there a diversity imbalance in the gender or ethnic composition of the board's membership? The recruiting panel will be looking to appoint someone who can bring the relevant knowledge, experience and skills, but it will also want to appoint someone who will share the vision and values of the organisation.

It is important to ensure that you can demonstrate that you understand the culture of the organisation and its board. Some boards have a charitable focus while others may be more commercially focused. Once you thoroughly understand what the organisation wants and needs, you should prepare to demonstrate what you can bring to the table that complements and enhances the existing board skills.

Review again the advertisement for the non-executive role to ensure that you can show that you bring the skills that they want. It is crucial to identify and prepare examples and case studies of what you would bring to the board. How have you made a difference in the past through roles you have held in the corporate world or in voluntary service?

The panel interviewing you will need to be convinced that you understand the strategy of the organisation, and that your views, visions and values are in alignment with theirs. They will want to hear examples of your leadership skills and your ability to hold executives to account. Describe how your unique experiences and skills fill any gaps the board has identified in its composition. Be prepared to discuss the vision, values and culture of the organisation to demonstrate how your appointment to the board would add value. Show that you have researched and understood the board's strategic objectives, the risks that they face and that you can make a valuable contribution to the future direction of the organisation.

NEDs need to be confident and articulate, and demonstrate that they will be able to contribute in the boardroom. A key factor that will convince the interview panel that you have these qualities will be the way you answer their questions, so keep this in the front of your mind on interview day. Be succinct without missing relevant information. There's no time for waffle!

Remember that you have done your research to show that you understand the organisation, its aspirations and its challenges. Show the panel that you have the requisite skills and experience to fill the role on offer. You need to demonstrate at interview that you can bring something to the table and you will be a valuable member of the team. You won't be the same as every other board member, but you will fit into the culture.

Commonly asked questions

Here are a few of the most commonly asked questions at interviews for NED roles.

Make sure you prepare answers for all these that line up with the research you have done on the organisation's needs, future challenges and culture.

- Why do you want this role?
- What challenges have you faced in organisations in the past and how did you deal with them?
- How have you influenced change or challenged the executive in the past?
- What mistakes have you made and what did you learn from them?
- What do you know about us?

A CEO who graduated from the EBM Programme and successfully gained an appointment on the board of an NHS trust after doing so had this to say:

"I had the pleasure of attending the EBM Programme facilitated by Karl George MBE. As someone who is a CEO, has had a career, and built up experience and knowledge at a senior executive level, the opportunity to learn more about this was too good to miss. It is a very useful programme for businesses and organisations that are looking at implementing board structure and responsibilities, and for those wishing to secure a NED position.

Karl's experience and expertise shone through on each of the programme days, beginning with the roles, responsibilities, the legal aspects and the liabilities; all explained with examples of good and bad governance, and the related experiences learned. He leads the various sessions in a clear, concise and helpful manner. The programme content included real life case studies spanning several years within Karl's career as a NED. This stimulated some interesting discussions where questions were posed and answered. The structure of each session was excellent and of a high standard, culminating in the skill set needed to be an effective NED with the possibility of securing a NED position.

Since completing the EBM Programme I was offered interviews with two NHS acute boards, of which I successfully secured the position of associate non-executive director for a West Midlands hospital trust board. As well as meeting interesting colleagues, this programme is a great way to understand compliance, personal capabilities and the skills needed to fulfil a NED role."

Phil Gayle, CEO

Final thoughts on preparing for your interview

So let's conclude this session with the three key points that will help you secure the role you want, backed by the views of people who actually sit on appointing panels.

1. **You have a strong track record of what this role needs to highlight your experience in the best possible way.** Carmen Watson, Chair of Pertemps, says: "...a strong and successful track record of achievement is good. This is less sector-specific now as mature firms look to bring in new ways of thinking through diversity. Financial acumen, entrepreneurial flair, personal networks and operational aptitude are commonly sought!"

2. **You need great people skills, so demonstrate this in the interview.** John Edwards, Chair of Midlands Heart Limited, says he is always looking for people with "Great people skills, who can deal with challenging people."

3. **Show them that you would fit in with the board's culture and values.** Bridget Blow CBE, former Bank of England Director, says the key to success is being a good fit: "If you fit what they are looking for, that's the way to get the job."

Peacock was someone who was always flattered to be approached by head hunters for roles. Now he and Penguin were both realising that being a 'good fit' for a board role was a two-way street. The role, and the business or organisation had to be right for you as well as you being right for the opportunity.

As a novice, Rabbit was delighted to have such clear advice on preparing for interview and was feeling more confident.

Bee enjoyed the structure of the advice and was ready for the final session of step three – more top tips.

Chapter Nine

Getting ready for your new role

"I feel ready **for anything** that an interview panel could throw at me now!" said Bee, almost bursting with confidence.

"It was certainly useful to end that section on preparing for an interview with real advice from people who sit on the panels that make board appointments," said Penguin.

Even Rabbit was looking happy: "**I do** have a strong track record and I can show it. **I have** got good people skills. **I will** find an organisation where I fit perfectly into the culture, the vision and the values!"

Peacock was quieter than usual, but eventually broke his silence to say: "I took a lot from the last session. We mustn't be afraid to say when we realise that something isn't a good fit for us and we should take ourselves out of the running."

When he realised everyone was looking at him in surprise at this change from his usual bull-like stance on things, he added hastily: "Of course, I knew that. I often turn down things that aren't right."

The Governor smiled. "You've really worked hard in these sessions on getting an appointment," he said.

"Now before we take a short break at the end of step three, I think it would be good to have a recap on all the issues we've covered in this section on seeking and getting an appointment. Are you all feeling more confident now about where to look and what to do when you find the appointment you want to secure?"

Peacock sniffed and said, a little reluctantly: "Yes, I suppose there were a few useful reminders of things I might have forgotten over the years."

"I thought it was brilliant," said Rabbit, eyes shining. "I'm really looking forward to working on my CV and putting all that information into practice."

"We're certainly going to be busy," said Bee.

"We certainly are," said The Governor. "So let's recap and cover a few top tips, and then we can all enjoy a well-earned break.

"In this session I also have some advice for you from another experienced non-executive, Greg Dyke, a British media executive, broadcaster and former chair of The FA."

Whether you are pursuing your first appointment, are just about to begin your first NED role or even if you have years of experience under your belt, these top tips from The Governor will help you ensure you are always at the top of your NED game!

The Governor speaks

Identifying a role

My first tip is to identify the board you want to join, and think how your background and skills will be of benefit to the organisation. It can't be all about what you want. You have to make sure you are targeting a board role where you can make a valuable contribution.

As I mentioned in the last session, former Bank of England director and experienced NED, Bridget Blow CBE told me: "[My top tip is] being a good fit. If you fit what they are looking for, then that's the way to get the job." She also warned: "You do have to work quite hard these days. It's quite competitive."

You will already be aware of the duties of a director, as outlined in the Companies Act 2006 and covered in Chapter Two. As a refresher, let me remind you that you have a fiduciary duty to the company or organisation, and a duty of care. This means that you must carry out your role with care, skill and diligence. You should also ensure that you avoid any conflicts of interest.

Be sure that you can commit the time required to undertake the role. There will be lots of information for you to read and digest between the actual board meetings.

As part of your research before applying for a position, visit the organisation's website and familiarise yourself with all the relevant background information, including the identities of the executive director and other board members. Read relevant industry briefings and publications for the sector in which your target organisation sits. After you have completed your initial research, list any questions that require clarification. Include any areas of concern you have or issues on which you need more information.

Carry out a self-assessment of your skills using the **6Cs** as a guide so that you are aware from the outset what your development needs are. The **6Cs** are **competence**, **commitment**, **contribution**, **comprehension**, **capability** and **code**. If you return to Chapter One, you can refresh the details of the **6Cs**.

Induction

Once you have received the good news that the role is yours, ensure that you receive a proper induction. This should include information and/or presentations about the organisation, and meetings with executive members of each of the key functions, where necessary.

It may be possible, before accepting the role, to attend a board meeting as an observer. This will help you to be sure that you are clear about how the board operates. Use the experience to observe how the executives and non-executives work together. Note how the meeting is chaired and the contributions of the board members. Consider how timely and useful the reports are that members have received.

As part of your induction, you should receive the legal and statutory information, including the annual report, the accounts, the constitution, and the board and committee structures. Ensure that you read all key documents, such as the risk register, the corporate plan and financial plan.

Make a note of the key corporate objectives, the key risks of the sector and the key risks of the organisation. Pay attention to all the key indicators including turnover, profit and balance sheet value. Also take note of the culture, vision and values so that you are well prepared for your role. You should seek assurance that accounts are up to date and there are no specific nuances in the articles. Review the terms of reference for the board and committees, checking boundaries and delegations.

Now that you understand the broad objectives and areas of risk you can take a more detailed look and get a view on inter-relationships between the documents. Look for evidence of how one document, such as the terms of reference for the board, informs the schedule of matters reserved for board consideration.

Request a copy of the calendar of board meetings and other events, such as away days and staff events, and add the dates to your diary. If you have any queries about the documentation, governance or any other information, now is the time to seek clarification.

Review your role description and terms of appointment. Sign the relevant paperwork, and complete all of the required forms and declarations, ensuring you retain copies for your records.

Preparation for meetings

When preparing for meetings, always ensure that you:

- Review the agenda and papers before the meeting.
- Prepare a crib sheet of key numbers and indicators to refer to until these key numbers become second nature.
- Make notes as you read the reports, remembering to check any assumptions made, clarify any areas of uncertainty or ambiguity, and looking out for unexplained variances or deviations from forecasts or plans.
- Make a note of areas that you are not sure about or need further explanation about. Remember you can request time for explanation outside of the meeting.

During meetings

Ensure your contributions throughout the meeting remain strategic and relevant. Remember that a key part of your role is to scrutinise and pay close attention to issues involving risk and financial control. Keep your questions and contributions clear and concise.

You can ask factual questions to clarify your interpretation or understanding. You can also pick up on points made by your colleagues and dig deeper to get to a suitable answer. There are no stupid questions, so if you are not sure of something, ask. However, this is another time to remind you of the importance of reading your papers, and doing appropriate background research on the organisation's history and the relevant sector/industry background. If your questions highlight that you've not done your homework, it will reflect badly on you and your ability to be an effective and high-performing board member. You can check on the expected outcomes from decisions made, or the impact or progress on previous plans.

When reviewing the remuneration policy and that of the executive directors, ask probing questions, request information about benchmarking and enquire how the outcomes have been linked to performance.

The way you conduct yourself at meetings is important. As a board member you should always display the Nolan Principles, which are openness, objectivity, honesty, leadership, integrity, selflessness and accountability. Chapter Four is the place to return to if you want to revise the information about the Nolan Principles.

Contributions

Some board meetings are quite formal, so be careful to observe board protocols, such as speaking through the chair. Don't speak for the sake of speaking, but do try to make contributions on all areas of business not just the area in which you have expertise. Contributions include asking questions and seeking clarification. Try to make your contributions in a way that stretches and challenges the executive as well as scrutinising performance.

Always think about how you are adding value as a board member. Your monitoring and compliance role is important, but also try to think outside of the box. Make yourself available for evaluations/appraisals and make a note of where you feel your performance can be improved. Also take notes and feedback as appropriate where board meetings, board papers or committee meetings could be improved.

Remember that you are an ambassador for the organisation, so be aware of how you represent the organisation, and be willing to open up your networks and make time to carry out visits with the various stakeholders, always talking positively in your circle of influence about the organisation.

Advice from Greg Dyke

I interviewed the British media executive and former chair of The FA, Greg Dyke, during my work with TGF and I'd now like to share with you some of his thoughts.

He has a very clear definition of the difference between good governance and poor governance, which is worth remembering as you start a new role on a board. He said poor governance is when something goes disastrously wrong and you knew nothing about it. Good governance is exactly the same except that you did know about it in advance. You were warned and you did the work that was needed. Things do go wrong, but good governance is all about knowing.

Greg told me that his favourite books on leadership are the works of Dr John Kotter, including *Leading Change* and *The Heart of Change* (27,28). Greg recalled that the Harvard Business School professor was the first person who explained to him the difference between management and leadership.

I asked Greg who was his favourite chair that he had worked with, and he said it was Sir Christopher Bland who was chair at London Weekend Television when Greg was chief executive and also chair at the BBC when Greg was the director general.

He explained that what was so good about Sir Christopher was that he made things move along quickly, and didn't suffer fools but gave everyone the opportunity to voice their opinions. He added: "You could argue like hell in the office but outside he always supported you."

There will be more about the role of a chair, and advice on how to secure an appointment as a chair, in Chapter 12.

Greg's top tip for getting a NED appointment is: "Choose what you want to do and hustle for it. Like anything in life you don't get it by sitting waiting."

He said you should find what you want to do and then start lobbying for it. This goes back to what we discussed in Chapter Seven about raising your profile. These days, most board appointments are advertised openly, and there is a fair and transparent recruitment process. You can remind yourself what we said about recruitment in Chapter Six. However, in these days of intense competition for board appointments, you need to work on your profile and actively seek out the roles for which you would be a great fit.

When you arrive at your first board meeting as a new NED, Greg's advice is: "Don't talk too much, but ask very pertinent questions."

Final thoughts

Being a new NED can be daunting. As a more seasoned NED, it can be easy to fade into the background.

Applying the principles I have covered in this session, with help from Greg Dyke, will ensure that you settle in smoothly and easily when you are new. If you have been on the board for a while, these top tips will help you stay current, relevant and effective. The key thing to remember is that, as a member of the board, you are responsible, accountable and a champion for your organisation!

Rabbit felt reassured when he realised that everyone else doesn't feel

100% confident the entire time, and was encouraged by the idea that when he achieved his first board appointment he would find other members and could start to form alliances to get things done.

Bee was particularly interested in the idea of having a plan at the outset for what she wanted to achieve during her term on a board. Perhaps just leaping in, and trying to impress by being active and energetic wasn't everything? It was now becoming clear that a calm, strategic approach would reap more benefits. She started to think about her legacy. What did she want to have changed as a result of her time on the board? She was going to give that some serious thought. It was never too late to make a plan.

Penguin could see from the advice that Greg Dyke had offered that taking a laid-back approach all of the time wasn't always the best idea. She was going to look harder for the opportunities where she could make a difference, the causes she felt passionate about and lobby to get those appointments.

Peacock was particularly influenced by Greg Dyke's comments about Sir Christopher Bland's approach to the role of chair. If someone like Greg Dyke was impressed by that approach then there were clearly things that Peacock needed to address in the way he behaved with his fellow board members.

The animals had now reached the end of step three and were now ready to embark on step four – how to be effective in the boardroom.

STEP 4

Chapters 10-13

What you do

Chapter Ten

Opportunities to shine and the link to good preparation

Penguin, Peacock, Bee and Rabbit had now covered all the aspects of seeking and getting a board role that suited their talents, skills and experience. They understood how to find the roles with businesses and organisations that they felt passionate about, or in which they were deeply interested.

They had taken on board all of The Governor's advice about having a plan for how they could make a difference, and how to raise their profiles in life and in business. The animals were now ready to move on to step four of the five-step plan. They would now be getting lots of practical advice about carrying out their role once their feet were under the boardroom table.

As they got ready for the first session of step four, Rabbit walked off to get another cup of coffee and could be heard repeating: "I do…I have…I will."

"You're sounding confident and powerful, there," said Penguin to Rabbit. "I bet you can't wait to get properly involved and make a real contribution at a board meeting."

Rabbit went a little pale and the smile vanished.

Peacock strutted across, chest puffed out with pride: "I love holding the reins of power! The board is where the **real** power lies."

The Governor looked across to Peacock: "Yes, the board does have the authority and responsibility of leadership, but real power takes many forms. Power sometimes lies with other stakeholders, including the client, customers or staff. The board should be aware of what power they really have, and exercise that power with the competence and skill required to ensure the board remains strategic."

Rabbit twitched nervously: "What about the executive of the organisation?"

The Governor smiled: "There has to be a good relationship between the board and the executive for an organisation to be well managed, and that relies on power being adequately balanced.

"The board has to get the balance of power right and work to its terms of reference. Executives and non-executives need to decide where the boundaries lie and what level of engagement is required with different stakeholders."

"I'm going to have to learn how to communicate and deal with lots of different types of people, aren't I?" asked Rabbit.

Penguin spoke reassuringly: "It's fine. I can get on with anyone. Go with the flow. You'll be fine."

The Governor stepped in again: "We'll have a look next at how the behaviour of people in board meetings impacts on the effectiveness of board meetings and how, if you are new like Rabbit, you can make the most of your contribution.

"However, even when you have been a regular presence at board meetings for years, like Peacock, there are still things you need to remember and apply.

"In the first session of step four we are going to look at how to be effective in the boardroom. Our second session will look at the roles of committees. We'll move on to look at board members' roles in session three and our final session in step four will look at how to evaluate your own performance."

Attending your first, or any, board meeting can be a daunting prospect but being equipped to contribute to that meeting can make all the difference. If you are an established board member, it's also important to welcome the contributions and questions from a new board member.

Let's hear from The Governor about how both **new** and **prepared** board members make board meetings effective!

The Governor speaks

First of all, what do I mean by a **new** board member?

I am imagining an addition to a board who may be younger, from a different ethnic background or gender to the existing board members. **New** board members could also include tenant members on a housing board or parent governors on a school governing body.

New board members bring a fresh perspective that is crucial in breaking the status quo of 'business as usual'. They may have an ambassadorial view, and represent the ideas and opinions of a significant group of stakeholders such as younger people, tenants or parents. Their input can help highlight gaps and risks, and contribute to setting the strategic vision of the organisation.

Imagining that first meeting

Let's picture what that first appearance at a board meeting might be like.

Imagine you have been part of a high-profile diversity campaign that seeks to improve recruitment processes and highlight the failings of a board.

The board you have joined has become susceptible to groupthink. In other words, they are all from a particular background or they have served together for a long time, and therefore lost the ability to demonstrate independence of thought and judgement. Your arrival on the board has been heralded as introducing fresh blood and a new pair of eyes. There's even been talk that you are the saviour of the board! No pressure then!

The board meeting begins and the usual formalities – apologies, approving the minutes and checking matters arising – have been completed. The first item on the agenda is a report from the CEO, which covers a number of strategic areas of the business, and triggers some debate and discussion. You haven't felt the need to comment until now, but there is a point you want to make. You raise your hand trying to get the attention of the chair, he or she notices you, and it's time to make your contribution.

It's as though the whole board is waiting to hear what you have to say. There is an uneasy silence while they anticipate what you will say. You make your comment, which is sound, valid and contributes to the agenda item being discussed. People nod, but it appears to be more to hurry along the discussion than in agreement with your comments. At least you have broken your silence and contributed to your first board meeting.

Usually, comments from a new board member are invited at certain points in a meeting. As the new member you bring expertise and experience in a particular area, but the board needs to understand that your role is much broader than that. Sadly, sometimes the new member's contribution is often only sought after important decisions have already been made.

In reality, of course, new members may not be excluded so obviously, but may well experience some of the pressures to perform that I have described.

So how can you perform as well as possible in the boardroom?

Four steps to being effective in the boardroom

1. First of all, ensure that you understand the key indicators about the organisation. I often say 'there is no such thing as a stupid question', but, unfortunately, there can be! If you don't read your board papers, or learn and rehearse the basic facts about what the organisation does, you may just ask a stupid question.

2. Next, remind yourself of the key corporate objectives and key risks that the organisation faces. Being aware of both the risks and the objectives will ensure that any decisions made aim to fulfil the objectives whilst protecting the organisation from associated risks.

3. Review the previous minutes. This will help you to identify contentious issues and areas that you need to keep under consideration throughout the meeting. Here, questions should be encouraged in order to ensure board members understand the decisions the board are making and why.

4. Finally, brush up on the list of questions that follows. You can keep these at the front of your mind in every board meeting to ensure that your contributions add value.

Budget questions

What was the process in pulling together the budget?

Was there a reasonable amount of diligence?

Are the assumptions reasonable and reliable?

How do the budgets compare to benchmarking? Are all covenants satisfied?

What choices/options have been rejected in pulling together the budget?

Are the budgets in line with the strategic priorities?

Performance indicator questions

What does this indicator help us to understand?

Does this indicator help me to carry out my role as a non-executive?

Are there too few or too many indicators to monitor the organisation?

How does this indicator compare to the previous period, other businesses in the sector or projections?

Are the indicators in line with strategic priorities?

What actions should management be taking as a result of this indicator?

What are the three to six key indicators to keep an eye on?

Balance sheet questions

Is the value of the business growing?

How easily can we meet current liabilities?

Are we reliant on loans to grow the business?

Are we holding large amounts of cash?

Income and expenditure questions

Does the service income cover costs (for housing)?

How do actuals compare with the budget?

Are overall management costs reasonable?

Are we complying with interest covenants?

Loans questions

How close are we to the covenants?

What would cause a breach?

How sensitive are we to fluctuations?

Do we have adequate draw-down facilities?

What is our treasury exposure?

Common themes in 'lessons learned' reports into failures

In recent years in the UK we have seen a number of independent reports produced following housing groups who have been taken to the brink of insolvency and banks that came close to collapse.

It is good practice to work through reports like these to ensure that we learn from them. Recurring themes we see refer to incorrect board composition and one specific example highlights companies who did not have enough independent directors.

If we are to avoid future catastrophes and near collapses, companies will have to take heed. As we say at TGF: "Governance is more than compliance." This was echoed by Chris Hodge, Executive Director of Strategy at the Financial Reporting Council, when he said: "To keep up the momentum of good governance, UK businesses need to move beyond compliance" (29)

I like the analogy of the thermometer and the thermostat when it comes to leadership. A thermometer records what is happening around it. It measures the temperature and says what it is. A thermostat, on the other hand, monitors what is happening and then takes action. It reacts to the temperature and does something about it, making the atmosphere cooler or warmer in order to reach a pre-agreed level.

An effective board member is like the thermostat. He or she understands what the organisation needs to achieve, and knows what difference they personally want to make. They take action to make things happen. When it comes to working with other board members, a thermostat board member will react to evidence of stress and bad temper by helping to cool things down. If things are getting cold and not enough is being achieved, they will see it as part of their role to get things back on track, and warm people up with inspiring and motivating contributions.

Every organisation needs to be sure that it has got all the basics of good governance covered. This means that they need to get the governance structures right, get the composition of the board right and take responsibility for the board's decisions.

Scrutiny needs to take place in many different formats. Typically, organisations have a number of stakeholders, all of whom should be included in the process of taking the temperature of the organisation. Board members must stay strategic, but site visits and interaction with staff, where appropriate, should be encouraged to get assurance and help them undertake their scrutiny role. This will not only help to inform board meetings and give board members real insight into how the organisation is operating but it will also increase the likelihood that they are fully aware of what is taking place in the organisation.

In the final analysis, it boils down to competency and behaviour. Boards need to ensure they have the right composition of non-executives with the right skills and experience who scrutinise, challenge and hold the executive to account.

The UKCGC sums up the responsibilities of the board and non-executives succinctly:

• "The Board and committees should have the appropriate balance of skills, experience, independence and knowledge of the company to enable them to discharge their respective duties and responsibilities effectively." (7)

• "Non-executive directors should scrutinise the performance of management in meeting agreed goals and objectives, and monitor the reporting of performance. They should satisfy themselves on the integrity of financial information, and that financial controls and systems of risk management are robust and defensible." (Supporting principle A4, UKCGC)

It is, therefore, important for boards to ensure that new members join regularly so that the skills and abilities of individuals are refreshed in light of the organisation's current and future needs. Every board should consider its succession strategy for the renewal and rejuvenation of the board. Boards also need to seek expert advice in a timely manner when entering into complex transactions, and ensure that there is a strong executive team and a second tier of management.

Final thoughts on being effective in the boardroom

A board must be made up of people with specialist expertise in key areas, who can operate collectively at a high level. The board should share a common vision and collective values. All members of the board should understand their duty to promote the success of the company and not just the individual stakeholder groups that may have elected them. The board and governance structure should be uncomplicated, and of sufficient size to embrace diversity but small enough to be effective and cohesive.

Is it time to take an objective overview of your board, its composition, skills, experience and its collective capabilities in light of the changing external environment? Is your board capable of undertaking oversight that is in line with the complexity and scale of the organisation that you lead?

Board behaviour can have an influence on the productivity and effectiveness of board meetings, and therefore must be managed well. This will ensure that board meetings do offer an effective place to monitor and control the organisation's activities.

Bee was very taken with the analogy of a thermostat and a thermometer. She realised she had been behaving like a thermometer and needed to be more proactive in making things happen.

Rabbit felt The Governor's list of questions was going to provide some strong support when he went into his first board meetings.

The animals were now ready to move on to the next session and look at the committee structures of boards.

Chapter Eleven

Valuing the assurance and independence of committees

There was a thoughtful silence in the room as Peacock, Penguin, Rabbit and Bee considered the information they had taken in during the first of the four sessions that would look at doing the job of a NED. The session on effective board behaviour had got them all thinking. Eventually, Bee broke the silence: "It's quite shocking to think how complacency has led to so many catastrophic failures by companies and organisations."

Peacock nodded thoughtfully: "I can see that complying with the law isn't enough. Good governance is about so much more."

Rabbit was feeling a little braver: "It's good to understand how I make my contribution in meetings. I feel more confident now, especially thanks to that list of questions. I am still a bit nervous about my first board meeting, but that session has helped me to understand how to prepare myself.

"If every board member does the same and if the processes to recruit members to fill skills and experience gaps on boards are robust, fair and open, we'll have the best people in the best places to challenge risky decisions."

The Governor raised his hand: "And that brings us nicely on to the next aspect of carrying out your role as a board member as we look at committees. What are the main committees you would expect to see?"

Peacock began: "Remuneration committee, nomination committee, audit committee, risk committee…We had a risk committee, full of specialists. No point having them and doing all the worrying yourself. Surely?"

Rabbit looked from one to another in confusion.

The Governor said: "I think we need to explore this in a bit more detail. Do we think it's a mistake to be complacent about the board's responsibilities around risk management?

"Is it still the board's responsibility to ensure that they carry out a robust assessment of the key risks and how to mitigate them?

"Specialists have an important role to play, but maybe board members can't wash their hands of risk management. What do you think?"

Rabbit sighed: "I need to be sure about what I need to be sure about. Can you help us, Governor?"

Preventing failure, which involves managing risks, is an important aspect of the role of board members.

The *Guidance on Board Effectiveness*, produced in the UK by the Financial Reporting Council (FRC), states: "While the board may make use of committees to assist its consideration of audit, risk and remuneration, it retains responsibility for, and makes the final decisions on, all of these areas." (30)

The Governor is going to tell us more about the guidance on how committees should operate. He's also going to take a closer look at risk management, so-called 'black swan' events and the **CORE** assurance framework – **compliance**, **organisation** and **risk,** and **effectiveness**.

Look out for one of the six most important acronyms in our five steps, **AIR**, which reminds us about the important role of the audit committee.

The Governor speaks

The major committees are audit, remuneration and nomination. The UKCGC says all boards should have all of these three committees.

Following the global financial crisis, most UK financial institutions will also have a separate risk committee. In other organisations, the audit committee will also look at risk.

It is worth bearing in mind that multinationals will have access to multiple legal experts and accountants, so they can create more committees, allowing them to separate the discussions. On the boards of smaller charities and organisations, resources are too scarce to have more than the major, prescribed committees. These organisations may only have access to one lawyer and one individual with financial expertise.

All committees should have terms of reference that clearly set out:

- **Membership**: Who can attend the committee? On an audit committee, for instance, it is essential that we have input from people who are independent. The terms of reference will specify how many people should be on the committee and, while the majority may be serving board members, a committee, such as audit, can include people who are not on the board.
- **Roles and responsibilities of the committee**: Can it take some decisions, or does it merely make recommendations? The FRC guidance notes on board effectiveness say that the board retains responsibility for audit, risk and remuneration – but it can choose to delegate power. This, however, does not absolve them of responsibility for decisions and actions taken.

Some organisations, such as the major UK retailer Marks & Spencer, publish committee terms of reference on their websites, which you can explore as part of your research. The minutes of committee meetings should be circulated to all board members, unless it would be inappropriate to do so.

Audit committee

We will spend more time on this committee than the others because of its central role in ensuring good governance.

The audit committee's role is described by the UKCGC in this way: "The board should establish formal and transparent arrangements for considering how they should apply the corporate reporting and risk management and internal control principles and for maintaining an appropriate relationship with the company's auditors" (7).

The acronym **AIR** helps us focus on the role of the audit committee.

A – Auditor: Audit committees oversee internal and external audits. The committee decides who the auditors should be and sets their terms of reference. The committee makes sure that both internal and external auditors are independent.

I – Internal: The committee reviews internal financial controls and risk management, unless there is the resource to have a separate risk committee.

R – Reporting: The committee will ensure that, when the annual report is produced, any narrative lines up with the financial figures. This means that you don't end up with a story being told about a successful year, which fails to address numbers in the annual accounts that tell a different and more worrying story. The committee must be completely satisfied that financial statements are accurate, and can stand up to scrutiny by shareholders and the general public.

AIR

Whistle blowing, health and safety, and conflicts of interest could also be addressed by the audit committee in some organisations. The audit committee should meet at least four times a year.

Before moving on to look at the roles of the remuneration and nomination committees, let's spend some more time considering the vital area of risk management.

Black swan events and risk management

The term 'black swan' was popularised after the 2008 financial crisis by Nassim Nicholas Taleb, a finance professor, writer and former Wall Street trader (15).

A black swan is defined as a random and unexpected event that has disastrous effects. The financial crash of the US housing market during the 2008 crisis is one of the most recent and well-known black swan events. It had a catastrophic impact around the globe.

Another example was the dot.com bubble bursting in 2001. At the time, the Internet was a relatively new phenomenon, which made the calamitous economic collapse that followed very hard to predict.

An effective board member will always be keen to ensure that failure doesn't happen on their watch. They will want to know that they are not responsible for the organisation becoming stagnant or losing its way. Preventing failure, identifying black swans or turning 'unknown unknowns' into 'known unknowns' is a vital aspect of the collective role of an effective board.

The audit committee, or the risk committee if there is one, has a core role in supporting the board to identify and mitigate risks.

The importance of being 'paranoid'

Risk management is a key component in the organisation's wider governance framework. Management control, internal control measures and oversight functions are the first and second lines of defence, and the board must ensure that it is confident that they work effectively. The internal audit function and how the board manages the function will then become an integral part of the management of risk. The audit committee is in place to examine issues in more detail and report back to the main board with recommendations.

There have been many corporate failures where the board was competent, and was provided with good risk plans and processes, but failed to gain sufficient assurance on many of the indicators that it was monitoring. The larger and more complex an organisation is, the more difficult it will be to get the assurance that a board member needs. Establishing a professional internal audit activity is a crucial part of the governance activity of the organisation, but board members need to ensure that they carry out their role.

Businessman Andrew Grove wrote the book *Only the Paranoid Survive*, which highlights the importance of being constantly aware that massive change leading to potential crisis is always around the corner (31). Grove, who died in 2016, was one of the founders and the CEO of the Intel Corporation. Under his leadership it became the world's largest computer-chip maker and one of the most respected companies in the world. In the book, he describes the moments in any business when massive change occurs. Every board member, he says, has a responsibility to consider the risk that sooner or later something fundamental in your business world will change.

Obtaining adequate assurance around key performance areas is something that board members should always be keen to ensure that they achieve. Board members not only help to set strategic direction and monitor organisational performance by challenging and scrutinising management, they must also find a way to gain comfort that all is well. To that end, it is advisable that they gain assurance in the following categories: regulatory compliance, organisational effectiveness and long-term sustainability.

In *The Healthy NHS Board [2013] Principles for Good Governance*, the NHS Leadership Academy writes (32) "...there is a growing understanding that robust assurance processes begin with the intrinsic motivation of the board to set, exemplify and monitor organisational values and fundamental standards, and support staff to deliver them. External regulation should be seen as a 'failsafe' rather than a primary source of assurance."

Board members and their boards should ensure that the organisations that they are accountable for are doing the right things, in the right way and, at the same time, have oversight of any potential risks.

The CORE assurance framework

Assurance can be obtained by developing robust and appropriate processes through an interrogative culture, and, as a result of a disciplined approach, provides enough evidence to comply with what I call the **CORE** assurance framework – **compliance**, **organisation** and **risk**, and **effectiveness**.

The framework is split into three areas, and aims to provide a logical and transparent means of identifying the criteria within which both the board and management will work. Let's look at each of those three areas and their positive outcomes:

1. **Compliance**: The organisation complies with its own constitutional requirements, legal and regulatory standards, and due care is exercised in maintaining the necessary internal control framework and proper fiscal oversight.

Outcome – the organisation is well governed and has an effective control framework.

2. **Organisation and Risk**: The organisation is achieving the best impact for its stakeholders within a pre-determined risk framework that ensures key organisational objectives are met and risks are appropriately identified and mitigated.

Outcome – the organisation is conscious, and able to respond to external and internal elements of risk, whilst ensuring that it maximises impact for its stakeholders.

3. **Effectiveness**: The organisation has a robust and relevant business-planning framework, and is led by an able and proficient executive team, who operate effectively against challenging and stretching performance indicators.

Outcome – the organisation is well run and with ambitious performance criteria being met.

Getting the balance right

An effective, high-performing board will examine each of these three areas and work with the executive team to ensure that they are provided with a rolling programme and evidence which satisfies them that the outcomes above are being met.

Getting the balance right in obtaining the correct amount of evidence to provide adequate assurance is never an easy task. In seeking to get too much evidence, board members risk interfering with the work of the executive team. However, seeking too little evidence leaves them exposed to criticism of lack of control.

In order to explain how to get the balance right, I have broken down the issue of obtaining assurance into three successive stages, three Cs – **comfort**, **confidence** and **conviction**:

Stage One: The board seeks **comfort**. At this stage there is a certain amount of evidence, primarily from the executive team, to demonstrate that the board is achieving the **CORE** assurance framework identified earlier.

Internal forms of assurance include management reports, management accounts, risk management reports and corporate reporting.

Stage Two: The board seeks **confidence**. Now, there is a great deal of evidence from a variety of sources and the board has put systems in place to ensure that the organisation is achieving its **CORE** assurance framework.

Independent forms of assurance include internal audit, external audit, regulatory review, inspections, quality accreditations and advisory services.

Stage Three: The board seeks **conviction**. The board now challenges the management and, where necessary, carries out 'deep dives' – rapidly immersing a group into a situation for problem-solving or idea creation to achieve adherence to the **CORE** assurance framework.

Combined forms of assurance that offer robust methods for gaining assurance include specific reviews, and triangulation of evidence across a range of assurances and assurance mapping.

It is worth noting that a board could never reach absolute conviction. The time and cost implications would be prohibitive, and would also lead to a level of detail not appropriate for board involvement. Having explored the **CORE** assurance framework and the three stages of assurance, board members will be equipped with a methodology to get the balance right in seeking assurance.

If the board finds it has an area to consider that will have a critical or high impact, it will look towards getting conviction, i.e. stage three assurance. An item that is less critical or impacting will only warrant stage one, or, in other words, boards only need to feel comfortable.

Remuneration committee

The basic principle that lies behind the remuneration committee is that directors should not decide on their own remuneration. This committee will look at major changes in employee benefits, as well as pay, performance and incentive schemes, and propose recommendations.

The UKCGC states that: "The remuneration committee should judge where to position their company relative to other companies. But they should use such comparisons with caution, in view of the risk of an upward ratchet of remuneration levels with no corresponding improvement in corporate and individual performance, and should avoid paying more than is necessary. They should also be sensitive to pay and employment conditions elsewhere in the group, especially when determining annual salary increases."

While not strictly an acronym, I am prompted by the first seven letters of the alphabet to remember the roles of the remuneration committee:

A – Appropriateness: Review the **appropriateness** and relevance of the remuneration policy, and determine and agree with the board the framework or broad policy for the remuneration of the company's chair, chief executive, the executive directors, the company secretary and such other members of the executive management as it is designated to consider.

B – Benefits: Oversee major changes in employee **benefit** structures throughout the company.

C – Consultants: Be responsible for the monitoring and recruitment of any remuneration **consultants** who advise the committee.

D – Determine: Approve the design of, and **determine** targets for, any performance-related pay schemes operated by the company and approve the total annual payments made under such schemes.

E – Expenses: Agree the policy for authorising claims for **expenses** from the directors.

F – Fair: Agree the policy for authorising claims for expenses from the directors. Ensure that contractual terms on termination are **fair** to the individual and the company, and that failure is not rewarded.

G – Guidance: Take into account all factors that it deems necessary, including relevant legal and regulatory requirements, the provisions and recommendations of the UKCGC, and associated **guidance** when reviewing and monitoring the remuneration policy.

The nomination committee

A main provision of the UKCGC says: "There should be a nomination committee which should lead the process for board appointments and make recommendations to the board. A majority of members of the nomination committee should be independent non-executive directors."

COSY is an acronym that reminds us of the role of the nomination committee:

C – Composition and **Committees**: Review the structure, size and **composition** (including the skills, knowledge, experience and diversity) of the board. Work and liaise as necessary with all other board **committees**, including with respect to membership of the **committees**. A clearly laid out formal letter of appointment is to include what is expected in terms of time **commitment, committee** service and involvement outside board meetings.

O – Organisation and **Other**: Review the leadership of the **organisation**, both executive and non-executive, considering the ability of the **organisation** to compete effectively in the marketplace and stay up to date on strategic issues affecting the **organisation**. Disclose any **other** business interests that may result in a conflict of interests.

S – Succession and **Skills**: Consider **succession** planning for directors and other senior executives, taking into account the company challenges and opportunities, and the **skills** needs of the board in the future. Evaluate the balance of **skills**, knowledge, experience and diversity on the board, and, in light of this evaluation, prepare the role descriptions and capabilities required for appointments.

Y – Yearly: Review, on a **yearly** basis, the time required from NEDs. Review, on a **yearly** basis, the results of the board performance evaluation processes.

Final thoughts on members' roles in committees

Well-informed and high-quality decision-making is a critical requirement for a board to be effective. Seeking assurance is a crucial function of your role as a board member.

Committees have an important role in supporting effective decision-making and good governance. The audit committee has a central role in ensuring good governance and the acronym **AIR** will help you to remember the focus of its activities: **auditor**, **internal** (control) and **reporting**. The board should be clear on how it will get assurance on the key strategic risks, and what type and level of assurance is appropriate.

Bee and Peacock were reminded again in this session of the importance of board members maintaining an oversight function. They must not stray into operational policy formulation and unnecessary detailed review, particularly where the item is not critical.

Equally, boards should ensure that management is aware that all board members need to receive accurate, timely and relevant information in a format that enables them to carry out their role and make good decisions. Rabbit had been worried about a lack of information, but now saw that a board should insist on getting the right information through to the non-executives. Penguin realised that, as a board member, it was her responsibility to ensure that she was fully prepared for every meeting and had read the information in good time.

Now it was time to look at the different roles that board members can fill.

Chapter Twelve

Extra roles – understanding the role of the chair, senior independent director (SID), company secretary and governance practitioner

"I'm feeling really fired up now to get out there and make more of a difference," said Bee enthusiastically. "I've been working on boards for a number of years – but this training is really waking me up to how boards can be **truly** productive and effective, and how important it is to get the balance right.

"I have always been diligent about rules and order, but I can see that it's just as important to make decisions promptly and decisively. Process is important, but there's more to it than that. A board has a clear role and so do the committees that support the board."

The Governor smiled and nodded: "Good. Good," he said encouragingly.

Penguin smiled and nodded too: "Providing you have a really good executive team who work well with the board, you have nothing to worry about. I think it's great when everyone gets on well. That has to be the way to go, doesn't it?"

The Governor looked round the room: "Do we think a cosy relationship between executives and the non-executives is the way to go?"

The smile faded a little from Penguin's face.

"Ha!" Peacock exclaimed. "Think you've fallen into a little trap there, Penguin. Challenge! Challenge and assert yourself."

A small voice piped up. It was Rabbit: "I think maybe there's a middle way, isn't there Governor?"

Rabbit stopped speaking as everyone looked across the room.

The Governor said encouragingly: "Tell us more about what you think, Rabbit."

"Well…" Rabbit hesitated and then carried on: "It's about balance again, isn't it? I can see that there has to be a good relationship between the executive and the non-executive board members. But if board members have to challenge the executive they can't be best friends all the time, can they…?"

There was another hesitation as Rabbit looked at the stern face of Peacock, then rushed on speaking more quickly: "But being a bit of a dictator who doesn't listen, and ploughs on regardless of whether you have all the facts and all the background knowledge is just as dangerous."

"Yes," said The Governor. "While good relationships should be maintained between the board and the executive, the board should not be afraid to disagree and offer constructive solutions that promote the success of the company. It's not just about the chair. We're going to look at the other key roles that exist on boards. Maybe this will whet your appetite to go for one of these roles in the future."

Bee smiled. She'd been looking forward to this session. She was so keen to get a role as chair and hoped The Governor had some specific advice to help her.

A reliable and competent executive team is a definite asset for an organisation and a fundamental ingredient for any successful company. But, the better the executive team is, the better the board needs to be!

Let's hear what The Governor has to say about the specific roles of the chair, the company secretary, the governance practitioner and the senior independent director (SID). He also has some thoughts to share from experienced non-executive Lord Ouseley about how to be a good chair. There's also the last of our six most important acronyms to look out for, **ABC LEAD**, which helps us remember the key role of a chair and the personal characteristics they need.

The Governor speaks

Executive teams are operational by nature, so you need to have a strategic balance coming from the board. The relationship between the executive and non-executive members is a fundamental part of a well-run organisation, but it is important to avoid a cosy relationship. Boards are there to challenge appropriately and if you have a good executive team, then a board that can rise to match them in skills, knowledge and expertise is critical.

The role of chair

Having a good chair is a critical part of ensuring that your organisation is governed well. Good boards don't happen by accident. Listen to what the FRC says in its *Guidance on Board Effectiveness (30)*: "Good boards are created by good chairmen. The chairman creates the conditions for overall board and individual director effectiveness."

In other words, the role of chair is crucial to the success of an organisation. Attracting and recruiting the right chair can be the best thing for your company. If you get it wrong, however, it can be the worst thing for your company, its reputation, the shareholders and anyone else involved!

We're going to explore some of the major issues experienced by chairs. If you have ambitions to take on the role of chair in the future, you need to be thinking about these issues in advance and considering them alongside some of the key principles of leadership.

Chairing is a role that carries a great deal of responsibility. Executing this role well requires the right balance of knowledge, skills and experience. However, if these elements are not appropriately applied, or if there is a misappropriation of skills, boards become ineffective and, in the worst scenarios, dysfunctional.

A chair should demonstrate the very highest standards of behaviour and lead by example. I want you to spend a few moments thinking about the behaviours and characteristics of a really good chair who you may have served, or observed, in the past. Now, think about those chairs who didn't perform as well. What can you pinpoint that made them hard to work with, or ineffective and unproductive? It's always really helpful to identify behaviours you have witnessed in board meetings. When I've run workshops with board members in the past, there are a number of comments that crop up time and time again, and these are listed as follows.

Good chairs:

- demonstrate a sound understanding of the organisation;
- encourage participation in decision-making;
- manage the dynamics of the other board members;
- follow the agenda; and
- ensure that every meeting identifies actions and ways to monitor the on going performance of the business or organisation.

Bad chairs:

- display a disorganised, dictatorial style or make meetings more of a social gathering than a place of business;
- lead meetings that are unproductive in terms of progress and decisions;
- preside over meetings that usually overrun, or fail to follow or complete the agenda; or
- are unclear on details and the latest information about the organisation.

The role of a chair is a challenge that no one should underestimate. Lord Ouseley, who has been at the forefront of campaigning to end institutional racism and chairs the Kick It Out campaign to end discrimination in football, had this to say to me about the characteristics of a good chair:

"A good chair tries to make sure he knows the personalities and the things that make other people on the board tick. You have got to get other people on side, but you've also got to have a talent to be consensual because where there are conflicting issues the decision might be confrontational."

Lord Ouseley added that a good chair has to find a way to get what they want and what they think is best for the organisation, but still manage to appease people who object. He said you have to have a talent to make people feel special even when they have not won the day and the decision has gone against what they wanted.

"That's a special quality in a chair," said Lord Ouseley.

I fully endorse that. That special quality of relational skills, the ability to bring people together – that's a really important characteristic for a chair.

As a chair, you are the first among equals, leading other people who are great leaders in their own sectors and specialisms. You need to find appropriate and productive ways to maximise their leadership skills, but you also need to cultivate a culture of teamwork. You have to be dominant without being oppressive. You have to be authoritative but not autocratic. You need to influence but not overpower.

In his book *Thin On Top: Why Corporate Governance Matters and How to Measure and Improve Board Performance*, author Bob Garratt (33) articulates these apparently contradictory requirements in the following way:

"The interplay of the powerful personalities around a boardroom table will always need careful handling. This is the chairman's job and it is a demanding one. While powerful personalities often enjoy controlling others, they do not enjoy being controlled themselves. Moreover, powerful personalities are rarely 'team players', yet a board is legally collegial and must learn to operate at the very least as an effective workgroup on the occasions when it meets."

Garratt acknowledges how complex the role of chair can be. Training and development in your role as chair is crucial to executing it well.

So, what are the attributes that make a good chair? You won't be surprised to learn that I have some acronyms to help! The first one is the **ABC** of a chair's role, which describes three important functions:

A – Ambassadorial:

- They have the ability to communicate with external and internal stakeholders.
- They protect the name and reputation of their organisation.
- They represent the organisation at functions and meetings appropriately, professionally and well.

B – Board:

- They properly address all major strategic issues.
- They carry out key board tasks.
- They manage the calibre and competence of the board.
- They maximise the relationship between executives and non-executives.
- They manage board business well, including sticking to the agenda and good timekeeping.
- They monitor how the board is performing.
- They engage with each and every board member, encouraging and empowering contributions and feedback.
- They provide correct and accurate information to the board.

C – Chief executive:

- They support the CEO.
- They define and determine boundaries with the CEO.
- They monitor the CEO's performance.
- They appraise the CEO.
- They liaise with the CEO to develop other directors.

The **ABC** (**ambassador**, **board** and **chief executive**) of an effective chair describes what they do in their role. But, to be a good chair, they also need certain personal qualities that contribute to how effective they are in the role.

The acronym **LEAD** helps us to remember these personal characteristics:

L – Legacy:

- They have personal integrity.
- They have intellectual capacity – understanding, thinking and reasoning.
- They demonstrate leadership – setting the vision and practising what they preach. It's important to consider what the outcome of your time as chair will mean for the audience. What is going to happen on 'your watch'?
- They think creatively.

E – Enthusiasm:

- They are persuasive, but still sensitive.
- They demonstrate leadership – taking the vision into the hearts and minds of people.
- They speak their mind.

A – Authority:

- They have the ability to influence others without dominating.
- They have confidence and presence.
- They maintain control without dominating or being autocratic.
- They have tact and diplomacy.

D – Decisive:

- They get things done.
- They draw clear conclusions.
- They show impartiality and fairness.

Company secretary

No one should make the mistake of thinking that company secretary is an administrative or clerical role. This is a role that focuses on compliance and legal issues, so you will often find it is filled by a senior figure with professional qualifications in subjects such as law or accountancy. In fact, the company secretary is on a par with the chair and the chief executive in terms of the importance of their role in running the organisation.

The duties of a company secretary include the following:

- Ensuring compliance with internal regulations and legislation.
- Maintaining records and managing access to them.
- Administrating the board and general meetings.
- Filing forms, etc. at Companies House.

- Collating accounts and ensuring compliance with legislation.
- Providing shareholder communications.
- Providing legal advice.
- Sharing administration.
- Ensuring the security of documentation.

One example of part of the company secretary's role is their involvement if a suggestion arises that a director has a conflict of interests. They will look at the declaration-of-interests form the director completed. They will ensure that this form is structured in a way to gather all the relevant information on any director's interests and investments in other companies and organisations. Company secretaries will also have input to the maintenance of a robust conflicts-of-interest policy, recommending and maintaining the procedure that is followed when an issue arises.

Minute taking is an important part of their role. The company secretary must attend all board and committee meetings (or have oversight of such), and has to make sure that minutes are accurate as they are important legal documents. It is a skill to ensure that the correct level of detail is recorded: not too much but not too little. Specific, tailored training exists to teach company secretaries how to take minutes that contain all appropriate details. In many cases it is sufficient to record that a particular issue was discussed and what decision was reached at the end of the discussion. However, sometimes there needs to be a more detailed audit trail describing the discussion to show how the decision was reached. Minutes of all meetings of directors must be kept for at least 10 years.

The company secretary also maintains registers, such as the share register, which records who shareholders are; a gifts-and-hospitality register; and the conflicts-of-interest register. An insiders' register would also be common in certain jurisdictions. They also have responsibility for filing annual returns and ensuring that the annual general meeting (AGM) is organised and run properly. They will handle all issues related to the UK Data Protection Act.

The Companies Act 2006 (4) decrees that the directors of a public company have a duty to take all reasonable steps to ensure that the secretary of the company is a person who "appears to them to have the requisite knowledge and experience to discharge the functions of secretary of the company".

Governance practitioner

I feel this is a vital role that should be focused on and I'd be happy if, in years to come, the initials 'GP' made people think first of governance practitioner instead of a general practitioner or doctor! In some organisations, the role may be part of the company secretary's responsibilities, or it could be a separate job.

A governance practitioner is the professional responsible for managing the governance function of an organisation, whether in a non-executive capacity, as a board member, as a governance consultant or in a direct managerial role.

The role of a governance practitioner is not limited to any one business function and practitioners are aware of their responsibility to ensure that good governance is part of how the organisation is run. The corporate administrator/company secretary will typically support these professionals, but, in most cases, they will have overall responsibility for this area.

Governance practitioners work in a variety of roles: some are consultants, and others specialise in risk or banking. What they all have in common is a strategic responsibility to ensure good governance.

The role may involve the following:

- Advising on governance structures and processes, and how they are implemented in an organisation. They will look at the committees and consider 'have we got the right number and are they the right committees?' They ensure that governance is relevant by taking into account the size, nature and key functions of an organisation.
- Ensuring that there is a clear understanding and implementation of the different functions of the board and of the management. Is the board following the governance code?
- Overseeing the risk management framework, and looking at appraisals and reviews.
- Contributing to strategic decisions and influencing effective board behaviour.

Senior independent director (SID)

In the wake of the Enron scandal in the US, Derek Higgs conducted a review of corporate governance. One of his conclusions, in 2003, was that the boards of publicly listed companies should appoint one of their independent, non-executives as a SID.

The idea is that the SID provides a safety valve. A key role for the SID is to be a sounding board for the chair, providing support – but they also lead the evaluation of the chair on behalf of the other directors and can intervene if an issue involving the chair arises.

The role of the SID becomes critical when the board is going through difficult times. They take a lead in resolving significant issues, such as:

- if a dispute arises between the chair and the CEO;
- if shareholders or NEDs raise concerns that are not being addressed by the chair or the CEO;

- if a strategy set by the chair and/or CEO does not have the full support of all board members;
- if succession planning is not in place; or
- if it appears that the chair and the CEO have a relationship that is too close, and other board members are being excluded from decisions they are making together.

The SID becomes the person a board member or shareholder can go to if they feel they cannot go to the chair with their concerns because the chair is part of the perceived problem.

Final thoughts on board member roles

If you are a chair, would like to chair a board in the future or have any sort of leadership responsibility, why not score yourself against the items that are listed under the **ABC LEAD** acronym and identify any development needs you may have?

You can also use the acronyms to assess the chair in your next board meeting. If the feedback is appropriately given, be it good or bad, this could lead to more productive board meetings, better organisations and, ultimately, good governance!

Remember the importance of the company secretary's role. They have a leading role in good governance by supporting the chair, and helping the board and its committees to function correctly and smoothly.

The company secretary may also carry out the functions of a governance practitioner or this could be another person. Their focus is to strengthen all the elements that ensure good governance, which includes overseeing appraisals and reviews.

The role of the SID was introduced following a number of corporate scandals, when it was felt that there was a need for an independent, senior figure who could be an alternative point of contact for shareholders and board members who have concerns they feel are not being addressed by the chair or the CEO.

This session had lived up to all Bee's expectations, and she was keen and ready to put the advice from The Governor and Lord Ouseley into practice. Peacock was reflecting on his past performance and had decided he'd definitely be scoring himself against the **ABC LEAD** acronyms, privately. He just wasn't quite ready yet to share his self-assessment with the rest of the group. But he might have to think about it even more because the final session in step four was coming up and that was all about evaluating your performance.

Chapter Thirteen

Reviewing your individual performance and that of the board

There was plenty for the animals to think about from the last sessions when considering how to be effective in the boardroom. The information on the various key roles on boards had been a useful reminder for Peacock, Penguin and Bee, and Rabbit had learned a huge amount.

The Governor told them: "We've now reached the final part of step four, which has looked at aspects of doing the job of board member and your contributions to the discussions have been very useful."

Penguin, Peacock, Bee and Rabbit had enjoyed a lively discussion about the behaviours of both good and bad chairs who they had all worked with or seen in action – or inaction, in some cases! Even friendly, easy-going Penguin had been encouraged to voice some honest opinions about bad chairs who let meetings ramble on without coming to a conclusion.

"It's **so** annoying when the squeaky wheels are the only ones who get the oil," said Penguin.

"Pardon?" said Rabbit.

Penguin explained: "I mean, there are certain characters who will talk and talk and talk until the cows come home. Everyone knows who they are. Other people might have really important contributions to make to a discussion, but they wait for ages and ages, and the chair never calls on them to speak. There are times when I just lose the will to live, and end up sitting back and letting them all get on with it."

Rabbit nodded: "Not everyone is naturally confident. I know I'm not. People like me probably need bringing into the discussions by a chair who can balance the needs of getting through the agenda alongside getting the best-quality discussion and feedback."

Penguin agreed: "The risk is that unless the meeting is well managed the board won't be in a strong position to make things happen or to take important decisions."

Bee, who everyone knew was particularly eager to become a chair in future, had been making notes against the **ABC** and **LEAD** acronyms.

Peacock looked across at the page as Bee scribbled furiously.

"Rating your performance there, are you Bee?" asked Peacock.

Bee looked up: "Yes. I think these acronyms are a great way to see quickly where I need development. I'm learning there's no shame in being honest about the areas where we can **all** improve."

The Governor stepped up and asked them: "So, when things go badly wrong, I mean really seriously wrong, what's the answer?"

"Sack the CEO and the chair!" said Peacock, scarcely stopping to think. "Problem solved. The buck stops with them."

"Wouldn't people in some of the other roles we looked at be able to help before things got to that state?" asked Rabbit. "The company secretary and the governance practitioner could help."

Bee agreed: "And if there were people on the board who could see things they weren't happy with, they could go to the SID if they thought the chair wasn't listening to them."

The Governor spoke up again: "Right, so for this final session in step four, on doing the job of a board member, I want to look at how we evaluate our own performance and how the performance of others on the board is scrutinised."

Problems that lead to corporate failures and scandals are often embedded in the culture of an organisation or company. Sometimes the solution can be as drastic as getting the whole board to stand down, and having a fresh start with a new chair and more effective, strategic leadership. There's a lot to cover in this session, so let's get started and find out what The Governor has to say about governance reviews, skills audits and performance reviews.

The Governor speaks

The UKCGC recommends self-evaluation, saying: "To enable the board to work effectively, they will periodically review their performance both as individuals and as a team." (7)

So, I want to look now at the different methods of audit, review and appraisal that will ensure that the board continues to operate at peak efficiency.

I'll talk you though various stages, including:

- auditing the skills of board members – initially through self-evaluation;
- mapping those declared skills in a matrix;
- following up with a reality check, seeking evidence and corroboration where necessary;
- identifying skills gaps and training needs;
- carrying out a board effectiveness review;

- carrying out a documentation review;
- carrying out a whole-board appraisal;
- individual board-member appraisals; and
- appraisals of the chair and the CEO.

A skills audit and matrix

Board members are asked to complete a straightforward exercise where they rate themselves against a range of skills as having low, medium, high or very high competence in the areas outlined. To help them and to provide some consistency, it's a good idea to set parameters. For instance, a useful measure of whether a board member's skills are very high would be having a professional qualification plus experience in that area.

The next stage is to map these self-assessed skills on to a skills matrix. This provides a starting point for a discussion. It's a useful overview that demonstrates where the board needs to be strengthened. Various codes of governance also advocate an audit of skills.

I once ran this exercise with a board where one member rated himself as very high for every single skill on the list. This leapt out at me when the results were mapped, and I knew he was either a most exceptional and remarkable person, or he was overly confident. So, I followed up and had a one-to-one meeting with him. I'm afraid to say he had clearly overstated his skills. I would recommend doing follow ups as necessary to corroborate the actual level of skill versus the self-assessed version.

The outcome of the skills report and subsequent discussions may conclude that the board needs to recruit a new member or two, or it might highlight that training needs to be put in place.

Board effectiveness review

A key way of reviewing the effectiveness of the board as a whole is a board observation. An independent, external person can sit in on meetings, and note who spoke and at what times. I have done this for many boards in the past and it becomes a concern when you are an hour into the meeting and, perhaps, three people haven't spoken at all.

The observation will also note how valuable the contributions are that members make. There's no value in speaking if you are saying nothing of merit or not moving discussions forwards. Have you had the frustrating experience of sitting in a meeting where people continually repeat what someone else has already said? A board observer should note the most valuable contributions and report back on things such as how effectively the meeting was chaired, whether or not the board papers were delivered in good time ahead of the meeting, and if it was it obvious that board members had read their papers in advance, based on their contribution and understanding of the items being discussed (or lack of it!)

Documentation review

The quality of the board minutes can be reviewed and doing so can help the board to identify if any members are not attending, which also acts as a good record evidencing what was discussed and the decisions that were made. In the UK, the body responsible for the regulation and inspection of schools, the Office for Standards in Education, Children's Services and Skills (Ofsted), looks closely at the minutes of board meetings, and will look for evidence of scrutiny and challenge to help determine if a school is being well run.

Other documents that should be reviewed regularly include the terms of reference and risk registers.

Board evaluations and board effectiveness reviews (BER)

A whole-board appraisal, which is part of a board evaluation, provides all of the members with an opportunity to assess how they feel the board is performing. Again, this is a subjective assessment by each member who gives their feedback on a number of issues using a simple scoring system. If someone rates every question with the lowest score of one, for example, you would probably want to interview them to unearth whether they have a valid reason for doing so. Consideration should also be given to whether this individual is a whistle blower or if the issue lies with them?

One-to-one appraisals

The UKCGC calls for the chair to carry out an annual, one-to-one appraisal with each board member. Objectives/targets and outcomes should be set at these meetings, and then followed up throughout the year to ensure that progress takes place. The danger is that, for many organisations, the objectives and targets set in appraisals are forgotten about until the next year's appraisal. Targets and objectives should always be linked to outcomes that can be defined, and measured and monitored regularly.

The chair should be appraised by the SID, or, in some cases by, the chair of the nomination or audit committee if there is not a SID in post. This will usually be via a 360-degree feedback session. This means that confidential, anonymous feedback is gathered from the people who work around them, and this is summarised into appropriate questions and areas for discussion to be used during the appraisal meeting.

What's a governance review – and what's not?

All these audits and reviews that I have described are key elements of a governance review, but they are not the review itself. Taking the opposite view would be like saying I have had the brakes and tyres checked on my car and, therefore, I have had a full car service.

I am by no stretch of the imagination a car enthusiast or an expert on the process of carrying out a full car service, but a quick Internet search showed me the key elements of a car service. I have amended the list, and summarised in parts, so please don't use it as a basis for your next car service!

Before I get into the detail, there are three things that I have noticed about the service of my car that I think every good review procedure should have:

1. An on-board computer warns me of any impending dangers to the continued safe driving of my car by the flashing of warning lights. This allows me to get help straight away. In a similar vein, every board should have a mechanism, perhaps a set of indicators or an internal audit process, that works like an on-board computer, keeping track and letting the board know if any urgent action needs to be taken.

2. My first service is carried out after a designated number of miles have been reached, or one year after buying my car. Once I reach this limit, I get an alert so that I can book it in for a service. This service is carried out regardless of how well I think the car is running. Although it is not a major service, it still needs to be done. Boards should be made aware that they should carry out an annual review of their governance, even if they think they are effective and operating effectively.

3. After the first service, and at some point around the three-year mark, I normally have a more extensive service where a number of the car's parts are replaced. Boards should have a comprehensive

governance review (externally facilitated where possible), with a robust documentation review and board observations every two to three years.

Board effectiveness reviews

At TGF, we use board effectiveness reviews (BER). Now, I don't want to over engineer the car servicing analogy, but I have broken this model down into the stages that I identified for the car service, plus a final stage.

- **Stage One – Pre-work inspection**: This is where the garage will check for any car body defects, look at the lights, tyres, etc., which could impact the basic safe driving of the car. In the same way, I want to ensure the board has all the tools it needs to operate properly. I like to carry out a preliminary document review, which includes a brief discussion about the frequency and nature of board meetings, and the size, expertise and composition of the board. The minutes and terms of reference for the board and committees are reviewed here. In much the same way, the pre-inspection work will help to indicate where further focus may be required in servicing the car.

- **Stage Two – Low level operations**: The garage will then check aspects such as the condition of the battery, level of anti-freeze, seat belts, air filter, fluid levels, etc. These functions are critical to the smooth and safe running of the car. If you want to ensure that your organisation is effectively governed, the next thing you will have to look at is the board members themselves, the meetings and compliance with governance best practice. To do this, I normally suggest that a basic skills audit of the board members is carried out to ensure that the core competences are in place. The diversity of background, skills and experience is also considered. It is also at this stage that the board should be asked to consider how the information it receives and the format of the board meeting agenda helps it, or hinders it, in carrying out its role effectively. The timing of meetings, frequency and members' attendance should all be reviewed at this stage. Finally, I like to carry out a review of compliance with a governance code and establish the evidence against the categories identified in the code.

- **Stage Three – Core operations**: This is where the garage will ensure that all of the key areas are checked; for example, the tyre-tread depth, brakes, suspension and steering. In our governance review, we now need to determine the capacity, competence and performance of the board. Is the board able to steer the organisation in the right direction? Can the members of the board put on the brakes when required? Just as a car needs good suspension for bumpy rides, you should consider how resilient the organisation is to internal and external influences on performance, sustainability and the achievement of objectives. Board members should have annual appraisals to consider their performance, and the results should be used to ensure that they have collective feedback where training needs are identified and also individual goals to improve their performance. Board members should also contribute to a more robust appraisal of the board's performance and the committee's performance. The discussion could be initiated with questionnaires, a workshop or a mixture of the two. What is important is that the results of the discussion form an action plan that the board can work towards achieving.

- **The final stage...road test!** The garage concludes its work by road testing the car, especially if any major parts have been replaced. The final stage of the governance review should also seek to get assurance that the board is carrying out its role effectively.

> An organisation may appear to have all the right documentation, have regular meetings and be fully compliant with the codes of governance, but, on further examination, just like a road test on your car, it could be revealed that things aren't running as well as you would expect. The final stage of the review should be a qualitative review of certain documentation. To get a feel for the content and decision-making processes, three or four sets of board minutes should be reviewed. There should be at least one board observation and committee observation. In a three-year cycle, some element of stakeholder feedback is also beneficial, as well as tracking the risk plan and corporate plans in terms of the attitudes, comprehension and behaviour of the board is also important.

I don't attempt to service my car myself. In fact, I would go as far as to say that I don't do anything except drive the vehicle and respond to the warning signals, prompts and alerts. I also have a satellite navigation system that helps me find the most effective routes once I know where I want to go. I am not suggesting boards have a hands-off approach to governance and let the 'governance experts' dictate every aspect. I am suggesting, however, that boards should make use of experts, and the tools and resources to help them to competently execute their role, which is to drive the organisation forwards to the destination that they have determined.

In their book *Inside the Boardroom – How Boards Really Work and the Coming Revolution in Corporate Governance*, Richard Leblanc and James Gillies state, in relation to board effectiveness, that: "…while board structure is a significant factor to consider in the establishment of an effective board, board structure, in and of itself, does not appear to be sufficient to ensure effective board performance, because structure does not take into consideration the competencies of individual directors and the manner in which boards make decisions – possibly the most important thing that boards do" (58).

Their board-effectiveness model proposes three key factors in this area:

1. Board structure

2. Board membership

3. Board process

I completely agree with the components of their model and would emphasise that board behaviour is a critically important component when reviewing performance.

The possible pitfalls of typical appraisals and reviews

Let's look at standard ways of carrying out appraisals and think about why some board reviews just don't work!

A number of criticisms are regularly thrown at standard appraisal methods and processes, including the following:

- Documented procedures may be non-existent and if they are in place, procedures are often inconsistent or not followed at all by the board.
- Boards are not always clear about what success looks like, they have no tools for measurement and they don't agree their objectives.
- Cohesive deadlines with appropriate time constraints are often not agreed, resulting in drawn out and sometimes incomplete processes.
- Monitoring mechanisms are not implemented to ensure board members are completing the process at appropriate times in the review cycle. When they are implemented at short notice, without proper preparation, they are ineffective.

- Forms and questions are often standardised, not taking into account the needs, culture or desired output of the organisation, rendering the findings irrelevant to moving the organisation forwards.
- Appraisals for the chair and/or chief executive do not reflect the objectives of the corporate plan. Sometimes assessments are not based on the skills outlined in the respective job description, making the assessment ineffective.
- Skills-audit forms are often basic, requesting only the confirmation of skills in common areas, but with no evidence of experience to verify how a skill has or can be applied.
- No appraisal report is completed following an appraisal; therefore, findings are not followed up.
- There is no integration between appraisal results and training needs when personal development has been identified.
- Solutions to any issues highlighted through the appraisal process are often generic and the support provided, if any, does not always meet the needs of individual members or it is delivered to everyone collectively.
- Boards do not, or are unable to, interpret the evidence from the appraisal process. They don't seek outside professional advice and/or there are disagreements about what the evidence suggests.

A lack of detail, challenge, alignment of corporate objectives or consistent procedures will lead to cracks appearing in the way the organisation is governed. It is often these small cracks that lead to the Fédération Internationale de Football Association (FIFA), Polly Peck or Enron-sized scandals that can have a devastating impact on a sector, or something like a global economic crisis that affects the entire world. So, when planning your board appraisals, beware of these things that have the potential to make your board appraisal ineffective.

It is always useful to consider 'lessons learned' reports in trying to determine how to evaluate your performance as a board. Let's take a look at the report conducted by Altair, a niche consultancy that was commissioned by Sanctuary Housing Group and the Housing Regulator in the UK to understand the issues experienced by Cosmopolitan Housing Group, which was on the brink of insolvency (34).

At the same time, let's consider two reports from the banking sector. Both were published as a result of a then potential collapse at the Co-operative Bank, one from Sir Christopher Kelly (35) and the other written by Lord Myners (36). The Co-operative Group commissioned Sir Christopher Kelly's independent review. The Co-operative Bank announced an independent review into the events that led to the announcement of its capital action plan to address its £1.5bn capital shortfall. Subsequently, Lord Myners was also commissioned by the board at the Co-operative Group to conduct a comprehensive review of its governance.

All of these reports followed the *Walker Review of Corporate Governance of UK Banking Industry*, led by Sir David Walker, as a response to the banking crisis and the simultaneous FRC consultation on the combined code. For the private sector, we already have a 'lessons learned' report in the form of the UKCGC, originally compiled in 2010 with several revisions having taken place since this time (7).

In the housing sector, the report by Altair on the Cosmopolitan Housing Group followed the inquiry into the insolvency of Ujima Housing Association in 2007 (37). Since then we have seen the introduction of the Housing and Regeneration Act 2008, and the Cave Review's recommendation of establishing a new regulator for housing. The Home and Communities Agency (HCA) took over the investment functions of the Housing Corporation in December 2008 (38). The housing sector's own governance code, then known as *Excellence in Governance,* was revised in 2010 (39).

As I review the recommendations of the reports from Kelly, Myners and Altair, more of the same comes to mind. Not meaning to undermine in any way the substance of these reports, I cannot help but think that if one were to examine the level of compliance to the UKCGC by the FTSE 350 (Grant Thornton FTSE 350 Governance Review), and extrapolate that to companies falling outside of that reporting regime, we may find that there are some recurring themes that need to be addressed. The biggest area of non-compliance in the Grant Thornton review relates to incorrect board composition and one specific example alludes to companies lacking sufficient independent directors.

Every organisation needs to go back to the basics where governance is concerned: get the governance structures right, get the board composition right and get the board to take responsibility for its decisions. In the final analysis, it boils down to competency and behaviour. Boards need to ensure that they have the right composition of non-executives, with the right skills and experience, who scrutinise, challenge and hold the executive to account.

As mentioned in Chapter 10, the UKCGC sums up the responsibilities of the board and non-executives succinctly. A structured and reflective review of compliance in line with the two extracts below is recommended.

- The board and committees should have the appropriate balance of skills, experience, independence and knowledge of the company to enable them to discharge their respective duties and responsibilities effectively. (Main Principle Section B, UKCGC)
- NEDs should scrutinise the performance of management in meeting agreed goals and objectives, and monitor the reporting of performance. They should satisfy themselves on the integrity of

financial information, and that financial controls and systems of risk management are robust and defensible. (Supporting principle A4 UKCGC)

The following key recommendations from the reports from Myners, Kelly and Altair serve to reinforce the importance of the two key principles of the UKCGC identified above. As we go through them, I have highlighted 10 bullet points to help you ensure that you are clear on the key components of any board evaluation and how any lessons to be learned can be taken into account.

1. **Cosmopolitan Group's recommendation**:

"Governing bodies must analyse the skills they require to meet current and future business needs and refresh skills at board level if necessary – even if length of service has not been completed."

When organisations enter into transactions (which may include those that involve taking on debt) boards must: ensure that expert advice is called upon in a timely manner and that there is a good understanding of what the organisation is trying to achieve, carry out rigorous due diligence on investors and actively monitor covenant compliance.

The board should ensure there is a strong second tier of management and a good succession plan so that the organisation will continue to operate effectively should the executive team be focused on other urgent issues such as mergers, service failure or other significant issues." (34).

The first four of my 10 bullet points are:

- Refresh the skills of the board in light of the current and future needs.
- Look at your succession strategy for renewing and refreshing the board.
- Get expert advice in a timely manner when entering into complex transactions.
- Ensure there is a strong executive team and a second tier of management.

2. **Myners' recommendation**:

"It has to produce a highly competent and qualified Group Board with independent non-executive directors who possess the skills and experience needed to exercise leadership and effective oversight of executive management running a business of massive scale and complexity, quite unlike any other co-operative business in the UK. Unless the Group takes urgent steps to reform its governance and generate sustainable economic value, it will run out of capital to support its business. Value creation is the prerequisite for the organisation's survival, for value distribution to members and for the furtherance of desired social goals." (36).

My fifth bullet point is:

- Ensure non-executives are skilled enough to lead an executive that is running a large and complex business.

3. **Kelly's observation**:

"Failures in board oversight are inevitable if the criteria used to elect its members do not require those elected to have the necessary skills…Sustained success requires effective governance. Effective governance requires a high-performing board. The composition of the Co-operative Board, and the limited pool from which its members were drawn, made a serious governance failure almost inevitable." (35).

The sixth of my 10 bullet points is:

- The criteria and process for the selection of non-executives must identify and ensure the inclusion of the necessary skills.

4. **Myners – the major governance weaknesses**:

"These include four particular weaknesses of the current board structure: (a) inadequate collective capabilities and experience; (b) a widespread failure to understand the distinctive governance role of the board, and a tendency for lay directors to act as delegates more than independent representatives; (c) a lack of unified perspectives and shared purpose, given the frequent divergence of regional concerns and pre-occupations; and (d) an excessively complicated structure with an unwieldy board size combined with gaps and overlaps in accountability with Subsidiary Boards and committees." (36).

The final four of my 10 bullet points are:

- The board must have adequate collective capabilities with specialist expertise in key areas.
- The board should have a shared vision and collective values.
- All members of the board should understand their duty to promote the success of the company and not the individual stakeholder groups that they may have been elected by.
- The board and governance structure should be uncomplicated, and of sufficient size to embrace diversity but small enough to be effective and cohesive.

How to carry out an effective CEO appraisal

The relationship between the board and the CEO can determine so much about the performance of an organisation. So why does something as important as the CEO appraisal process often get carried out without the required care and diligence?

The appraisal of the CEO is a key part of the board's responsibility and the chair must ensure that this function is performed on behalf of the board in an effective and timely manner each year. CEOs largely look forward to the encouragement and support they receive for a job well done, and welcome feedback about how they can improve their performance; an appraisal to give a 'well done' – when it is deserved – can help to facilitate that.

There must be two-way communication between the chair and CEO, with honest, open dialogue and, when necessary, difficult conversations need to be had. The appraisal forms that are used are important and must ask the right questions, but a process that is not transparent, or where there is lack of trust, may mean that any feedback that is gleaned can be redundant.

An annual appraisal can take the form of an informal chat between the chair and CEO, particularly if they are already meeting on a regular basis. However, even in those circumstances, a robust documented framework for the whole appraisal process should be followed. There is no excuse for not appraising performance, but there are still a great many organisations that don't carry out appraisals effectively. As the saying goes: 'you can't manage what you don't measure'.

A good appraisal process will be planned well in advance and contributors to the process will be well versed in what is required. The CEO will leave the process with clear feedback about their performance, measured against unambiguous goals that correspond with the corporate goals and the CEO's job description. A bad appraisal process will be carried out as a 'tick box' exercise without due consideration being given to ensuring the performance measures are relevant.

The best organisations and their boards see the appraisal process as more than an annual feedback meeting. It is part of the process of engaging with the CEO to challenge, stretch and develop them, as the organisation too can be challenged, stretched and developed. This will mean that the performance matrix for the CEO will be more sophisticated than just the financial metrics, and links will be made to the outcomes and real impacts for beneficiaries. Performance will include achieving corporate plans and objectives whilst pursuing value for money.

A high-performing board will want to ensure that it sticks to its strategic role, but, at the same time, it must be confident in its ability to ensure that the organisation is performing well. To achieve this, it will be necessary for the board to hold the CEO accountable for the performance of the executive team.

CEO appraisal checklist

The following checklist will help you plan your CEO appraisal process:

1. Review the CEO's job description and performance measures, and determine who should input to the appraisal process.

2. Have regular meetings with the CEO to get two-way feedback regarding on going goals.

3. Agree dates for the annual performance review meeting and board meeting at the beginning of each year, and add to the annual calendar.

4. Meet with people who will complete the appraisal forms to explain the importance of and criteria for completing the appraisals.

5. Send out appraisal forms to the CEO and board members with enough time to complete them (I recommend at least 14

days). A full 360-degree review should also be carried out every three to five years, which covers leadership competences.

6. Collate all responses from the appraisal forms into a consolidated report and forward the consolidated report to the chair.

7. Arrange a meeting with the chair to review the information from the aggregated appraisals that have been pulled together in the consolidated report.

8. Carry out the appraisal meeting and get feedback from the CEO, review previous goals, set new goals, and agree development areas.

9. Present the highlights from the appraisal meeting to the board at a designated board or committee meeting, together with the agreed targets for the CEO.

10. Evaluate the process and make recommendations for improvements to the process for the following year.

Final thoughts on the evaluation of your performance

We all want to see organisations achieve the goals that they have set collectively. It is the responsibility of the board to set the vision and strategy, but this can't be done without the input of the executive. So, boards need to scrutinise performance and challenge the executive, but they need to be careful in how they do this by engaging with the CEO. A robust CEO appraisal process can help if it is properly conducted.

I would suggest that the entire evaluation cycle I have described should be spread out over three years. The importance of reviews and appraisals is that they identify opportunities to fill gaps in diversity, skills and experience. It can identify training needs and show how to maximise the skills of existing board members.

The **6Cs** that we talked about back in Chapter One can help shape discussions during one-to-one appraisals with the chair. The review process can identify areas of weakness in the board, and support the process of renewal and succession. It's essential that every board has written a succession plan.

All the review and audit exercises can feed into a governance action plan. The UKCGC says that every two or three years you should get external, independent help, as it's unlikely that you can remain objective all the time. The report isn't the answer even if it is put together by consultants. We have to discuss the report as a board and collectively formulate a plan. Once these steps and considerations have been taken, we've completed a governance review.

It had been a long session, and, for Rabbit in particular, there was a lot to take on board. Peacock had years of experience, but has still learned a lot of lessons he'd forgotten (or ignored) down the years.

Penguin resolved to buckle down and take a more proactive stance on evaluation. Bee was finding that things were falling into place, and she was ready to be open at her next appraisal and make changes in order to be more effective. Step four was now complete and the animals were ready for the final step of their training, which would pull all the previous sessions together and help them to be able to put what they had learned into practice.

STEP 5

Chapters 14-15

High-performing board members

Chapter Fourteen

Never underestimating your role and the critical issues that affect boards

It was nearly time to start the final step of the EBM Programme and look at how to put everything that had been learned in the first four steps into practice. But, first, The Governor encouraged the animals to reflect on the previous session about performance reviews and evaluation.

"How do you feel now about reviewing the performance of your CEO and your board?" The Governor asked them.

"Well," said Peacock, "There's lots of food for thought there. I will definitely be taking that back and looking again at the processes we have in place."

Bee smiled: "I just want to say that the latest sessions have not put me off from aiming to be a chair in the near future. I think I can bring a lot to the role and I'm getting such a good feel for achieving the right balance between rules and order, and being able to respond with agility and speed when necessary."

Penguin nodded in agreement: "So many things come back to having the right people in place on your board, and that means carrying out skills audits and looking at issues such as diversity of life experience as well as specialist knowledge. Personal qualities matter too. I'm coming to see that it's not about being everyone's friend all the time."

Rabbit looked a bit distracted.

"What is it, Rabbit?" asked The Governor.

"I'm just worrying about when my next car service is due. I'm sure my oil light was on this morning," Rabbit replied.

Bee laughed, but added: "That was a really good analogy though and it does make it clear how the right checks and processes are essential."

"So what's next?" asked Peacock.

The Governor replied: "It's hard to believe, but we're nearly at the end of our time together. But what I want to do in the last few sessions is to discuss with you some trends in corporate governance, and my own thoughts and experiences. We live in a fast-moving world where change happens overnight. There are always new tools, trends and technologies that affect the way we need to work.

"I always enjoy reading the views of corporate governance commentators and I believe that every board should be aware of what's happening in the world of corporate governance. So, we're going to look at four critical areas in this next session:

"Issue 1: Dealing with your regulator.

"Issue 2: Board composition and succession.

"Issue 3: Keeping up with technology and social media.

"Issue 4: Identifying risk and getting assurance."

"Buckle up," laughed Peacock. "This is going to be a busy session! Let's go!"

Let's think of these next few sessions as revision. We're going to take a step back, and look in a bit more depth at some of the issues around good and poor governance, putting together the right board, risk and assurance.

Here's what The Governor thinks about four of the critical issues that all NEDs should keep at the front of their minds.

The Governor speaks

Dealing with your regulator

"The ability to meet current and future regulation is hampered by lingering uncertainty over regulatory details and the potential for reactive and piecemeal implementation," said Kevin Burrowes, UK Financial Services Leader at PwC (40).

His comment followed a report about the top risks for businesses in the banking and capital markets. Over regulation was at the top of the list and this could be could be equally applicable across many other sectors.

Getting the relationship right with your regulator should be one of the key concerns of any board. If you don't understand the impact that they can have on your organisation and how you need to adhere to whatever regulatory guidelines they impose, then you are not in a position to have an appropriately balanced relationship. I am not suggesting that you should operate just to satisfy the regulator, but a by-product of good governance and a robust, well-documented assurance framework should be a happy regulator.

Unfortunately, it is not always that easy. In our complex and uncertain business environment, having a robust strategy around regulatory intervention and dealing with the burdens of regulation is a now a necessary board agenda item. It doesn't matter whether you are in the private, public or voluntary sector, regulators can have a disproportionate amount of influence on the running of your organisation.

I have seen across all sectors the pressure under which the regulators themselves operate. They are being called to account for businesses that they have been set up to regulate. When the regulator is under pressure, it's a natural response for them to pass on some of this pressure to the organisations they scrutinise.

In my opinion it's clear that they understand that their overall objective is to safeguard taxpayer's money, and respond to ineffective, inefficient and, sometimes, illegal practices. However, they are not always so clear on how to do this without being over-burdensome to the organisations and businesses that they monitor. Regulators are there to maintain standards and the reputation of the market segment for which they are responsible. But they also have to be more efficient, as their staff numbers are reduced and costs are cut.

In theory then, a co-regulatory environment would seem to be a logical answer and a risk-based approach to monitoring would be the way forward for regulation. The burden and responsibility for failure rightly rests with the board, which is collectively responsible for its decisions and actions if things go wrong. If they work outside the guidelines or best practice…woe betide them!

Thinking about this practically, local-authority-controlled schools in the UK have been converting to academies in droves. Outside of local-authority influence, they have almost complete autonomy to operate as they want. But beware of Ofsted, the regulator for education, and the Ofsted inspector who has had the latest briefing on the latest topical issue arriving at your school to nip it in the bud.

With so many recent examples of failure in the provision of healthcare you can expect the UK's Care Quality Commission, the quality and safety regulator, to have a sometimes steadfast approach. Monitor, the sector regulator for health services in England, shares similar anxieties when working with bodies to ensure they do not let another scandal happen on their watch.

When the Inland Revenue gets a public vote of no confidence for its track record in collecting tax from some big corporations and those perceived to be rich business people, you can just see the repercussions for the small and medium businesses that have next to no resources to argue their case.

Finally, I would suggest that well-meaning and unsuspecting small charities, who aren't well versed in every regulation, are likely to fall foul of the Charity Commission – especially in the wake of a heavily-publicised charity scandal.

I could go on, but I am sure you get the picture.

So what can boards do?

My advice to boards that need help to avoid the wrath of the regulator is to:

- develop a proactive approach to regulation – take it seriously;
- ensure there is a senior leader responsible for co-ordinating regulatory liaison;
- review any updates to regulatory compliance that have been issued and become part of the consultations carried out by the regulator;
- update your monitoring and assurance protocols to satisfy yourself that you have all the bases covered; and
- review case studies and the experiences of others in your sector.

Board composition and succession

My second critical area for all boards to consider is the composition of the board. Every board should have the appropriate balance of skills, experience, independence and knowledge.

- "There is a strong business case for balanced boards. Inclusive and diverse boards are more likely to be effective boards, better able to understand their customers and stakeholders and to benefit from fresh perspectives, new ideas, vigorous challenge and broad experience." (Lord Davies (41)).
- Company boardrooms are still overwhelmingly being run by white men. In a bid to combat the low ethnic diversity, the then business secretary, Vince Cable, launched The 2020 Campaign. The aim is for there to be no FTSE 100 companies with all-white boards by 2020 (42).
- The Charity Commission estimates that only 0.5% of the trustee population is made up of 18 – 2 4 year olds and the average age of a trustee is 57 (43).

In 2011, Lord Davies set a target that by 2015 at least 25% of board members should be women. By 2013 the number of women on UK boards had doubled. The original target was reached by 2015 and the goal for the percentage of woman on boards was reset to 30% (44).

The 2016 Parker Review wants all PLCs to have at least one black and minority ethnic (BAME) person on their boards. Currently only 1.4% of UK board members are BAME, although they make up 14% of the country's population (45).

The evidence shows that diverse boards produce better performance, with many reports showing strong evidence for improvements in performance when women join boards. I am proud to have launched the Diversity in the Boardroom Campaign, which is aiming to bring change to boardrooms across the private, public and voluntary sectors in the UK.

There are many boards that have experienced members who know the organisation, and have great professional and board skills, but have served far longer than most people would consider best practice. Independent challenge and scrutiny becomes more difficult the longer you serve in any role. In addition, being able to think outside the box or bring an outsider's perspective becomes almost impossible. If you have not worked at an executive level for some time, it could mean your professional and sector knowledge is out of date.

All directors should be submitted for re-election at regular intervals. It stops the board becoming stagnant. There are different maximum terms in schools and the housing sector, for example. I know of one charity board that celebrated the 25th anniversary of all its trustees. The record I have come across so far was a NED who had been in post for 42 years!

The UKCGC says that any term beyond six years for a NED should be subject to particularly rigorous review. There are also provisions in the code that define whether a NED is independent. If a NED has served on a board for more than nine years, they are not considered to be independent. Except for smaller companies, at least half the board – excluding the chair – should comprise NEDs who are determined by the board to be independent. A smaller company should have at least two independent NEDs.

The opposing view is 'If it ain't broke, don't fix it'. When a board seems to be working well, and the organisation is meeting the corporate objectives and hitting its KPIs, then why worry? We are all aware of the concept of groupthink, which has the potential to stagnate ideas, challenge and scrutiny if it is allowed to direct the behaviour of a board. A groupthink culture is bound to lead to poor decision-making and bad governance when timid board members cannot express their views against the might of the majority.

Every board needs a succession plan derived from a succession strategy. This strategy can be developed by thoughtful investigation and consideration of the corporate objectives, future plans of the organisation, current strengths of the board, and external influences on the organisation. Replacing key board members will need organisations to think about their pipelines for developing and recruiting talent to ensure they can fill vacancies as they arise with competent and diverse board members.

Keeping up with technology and social media

According to the Institute of Risk Management, cyber risk is defined as: "...any risk of financial loss, disruption or damage to the reputation of an organisation from some sort of failure of its information technology systems" (46).

Don't make the mistake of thinking that you have to be Sony Pictures to be exposed to a cyber risk! Do you recall the group calling itself Guardians of Peace (GOP) and demanding that Sony's controversial North Korean comedy *The Interview* be pulled from release (47). At the time, *The Guardian Online* reported that the then FBI Director, James Comey, stood by the conclusion that the North Korean government was responsible for the mammoth computer hack on Sony Pictures, saying the hackers "got sloppy" and allowed their location to be identified on a number of occasions.

You could be exposed to a cyber attack for direct financial gain or non-financial reasons, such as stealing data or know-how, or to cause reputational damage or ridicule. Fraud continues to be a major threat to businesses, but the nature of such crime is changing. As essential business processes and functions are increasingly run through digital systems, as business records are increasingly kept electronically and as the use of mobile technology soars, businesses need to be prepared to match their investment in digital technology with the required investment in the appropriate level of IT security.

As a board member, you need to be aware of the impact of technology. The concept of cyber risk is one of seven digital-disruption demands (DDD) that I want to share with you. All companies, from large corporate entities to small businesses, are affected by quantum changes and shifts in technology.

"New digital business models are the principal reason why just over half of the names of companies on the Fortune 500 have disappeared since the year 2000." (48)

I would suggest that you take each DDD, and ensure that your board has considered the implications, associated risks and plans for dealing with them. But, firstly, I would encourage you to ensure that you are comfortable with answering these three questions:

1. Is your organisation's technology strategy integrated with your corporate strategy?
2. Does your organisation have a disaster recovery plan and is it prepared for the impact of failure in technology?
3. Do you have a plan for how your organisation will enhance its performance by maximising its technology capabilities?

So, now, let's look at the seven specific DDD areas that I believe your board should focus on:

1. **Rate of change**: It is because of the rate of change in new technologies and the speed at which expertise in this area becomes out-dated, that boards need to be digitally aware. Boards need to get assurance that their technology is capable of dealing with the demands of the organisation, the threat of cyber attack, and how it benchmarks against peers, competitors and the supply

chain. They should ensure that the chief information officer or equivalent is up to date with current thinking, and has a plan to keep all staff on a cycle of learning and continuous development.

2. **Customer experience**: Technology has transformed the customer experience in all sectors and, even if the sector you operate in hasn't caught up yet, you will be impacted. If your customers are used to a level of service in other areas of their life, they will come to expect it in all areas. Boards need to consider how they are able to ensure that digital inclusion translates into an enhanced experience for their customers. Each organisation should be seeking to 'disrupt' current service provision by the application of appropriate technology for the benefit of customers.
3. **Service delivery**: The way services are delivered has been completely overhauled in many businesses, so isn't it time to get your organisation on to modern platforms? The use of tablets, cloud technology, and the relatively inexpensive costs of either accessing mobile phone applications or developing them should help your organisation to deliver services in a more effective way.
4. **Social media**: Technology has transformed the speed, spread and nature of communication. Brand impairment, and mitigating and managing reputational risk should be as much a part of the board discussions as developing market profile and presence.
5. **Cyber risk**: Organisations need to learn to view the world from a cyber perspective and understand that cyber risk is never just a matter for the IT team.
6. **Data analysis**: The collection, storage, interpretation and use of data is a key tool for every board. KPIs should be developed in order to measure, monitor and control value-added activities, health and safety aspects, and financial and operating performance. The availability of relevant corporate data is a prerequisite for board members carrying out their role.

7. **Data security**: Breaching data security protocols can lead to legal consequences for your organisation. These include enforcement action from the Information Commissioner's Office under the UK's data protection laws. Further strengthening of the law in this area will take place subsequent to the publishing of this book. There are many examples in both the private and public sectors of organisations falling foul of losing customer or personal information.

In conclusion, you may want to consider how knowledgeable you are as a board about digital technologies. Do you understand the risks and implications of digital disruption, and what plans do you have to mitigate them? Have you spent enough time ensuring that you have considered the opportunities available to you by embracing the digital revolution?

Identifying risk and getting assurance

I've already made it clear that I believe a key role of a board member is to understand their role in monitoring strategic risks. Don't forget that the risk of not achieving an objective, e.g. maximising profits or income, is as much a consideration as the risk of potential losses or failures.

If you've successfully got a grip of your role in monitoring risks, you need to focus on how you scrutinise and challenge to ensure that you get the required level of assurance. In my professional opinion, the ability to identify risks before they arise and have a strategy for dealing with them is what sets great boards apart from good boards. I don't mean just the risks associated with preventing losses, but also the risks associated with new opportunities. As the UKCGC puts it: "The board is responsible for determining the nature and extent of the significant risks it is willing to take in achieving its strategic objectives." (7)

High-performing board members don't just rely on sophisticated metrics, quantitative measures and historical data to manage risk; they are able to do so much more. Great boards have mastered the **art** of risk management as opposed to the **science** of risk management. They have a 'soft approach' as well as a 'hard approach'. But, before I explain what I mean, let's quickly explore the basic principles of good risk management.

A good board will have a robust and systematic process for risk management, i.e. risk identification, risk assessment, risk planning and risk monitoring. They will spend some time determining their risk appetite and, by assessing the impact and the probability of risks that have been identified, they can come up with a register or action plan for dealing with risks.

The process may involve the **TARA** strategy:

T – Transfer the risk: A common example is insurance. Alternatively, we can **share** the risk, through a joint venture, for example. In that case, the **TARA** acronym would become **SARA**.

A – Avoidance: Not doing the risky activity.

R – Reduce/mitigate the risk: By pooling or hedging risks.

A – Acceptance: where the adverse impact is marginal you may decide to accept that the risk may occur and deal with the consequences if and when they arise.

All boards should make use of the tools and techniques available to determine and monitor risks. These include:

- **PESTEL analysis**, which looks at external factors, and analyses the impact they have on the business.
- **Porter's five forces**, which analyses five forces that determine competitive intensity, and therefore the attractiveness of an

industry. They are supplier power, threat of new entry, buyer power, threat of substitution and competitive rivalry. An 'unattractive' industry is one in which the combination of these five forces acts to drive down overall profitability.

- The **McKinsey 7S framework**, which says that there are seven internal aspects of an organisation that need to be aligned if it is to be successful. They are strategy, structure, systems, skills, style, staff and shared values.

The danger with all of this is that boards can get caught up in the tools and underestimate the importance of their role. Non-executives sit on boards to bring an independent point of view, an understanding of the wider business environment, and a broader perspective and insight.

Although necessary, the problem with the traditional frameworks is that they can force the board to miss the bigger picture. Boards can become complacent because they have ensured that they are confident that all the significant risks have been identified and monitored, and are captured on the risk map. They are encouraged to believe that things must be okay. But these frameworks can't deal with the unpredictable because, by their nature, they focus on risk events. Strategic risks, by their nature, are, for the most part, unpredictable because they do not fall into a simple, linear model. By focusing on specific events, boards can sometimes over-simplify what can be quite complicated and interrelated circumstances.

I am not suggesting that boards can predict the unpredictable, but an experienced and mature board will be able to detect clues that indicate impending dangers. It does this through a combination of sector or industry knowledge, organisational intelligence and depth of understanding of key issues, together with board members who work well together as a team. The ability to see the big picture, rather than focusing on events in isolation, is a skill that the best boards develop.

A board can never be 100% sure that it will get the balance right between risks that it can ignore and those that it needs to be 'all over'. What board members must be able to do is get enough assurance in order to make the right decision.

Don't get bogged down with colour-coded, red-amber-green (RAG)-rated matrices and tools. The tools can't make the decisions for the board. Good, old-fashioned common sense; intuition; an in-depth understanding of the environment in which the organisation operates; and interpretation of information are the skills that a board needs. When that is right, a board will be able to determine what to act on and what to ignore.

Final thoughts on critical issues to consider

If you haven't had a serious discussion on your board about the importance of staying on the right side of your regulator, cyber risk and the impact of the composition of your board, now is the time!

Let's all commit to regularly reviewing the skills that we need to have, and how much experience and in what sectors, including organisational knowledge, but also provide space for the development of creative thought, new ideas and diversity. Great boards don't do risk management solely as a separate exercise that falls on the board agenda or in the cycle of board meetings. Risk management is the *raison d'être* for the meetings and every agenda item forms part of the complex decision-making criteria that the board should be analysing.

I sometimes use the analogy of Iron Man, the fictional super hero, to describe an effective board member. Imagine that the board member has a powered suit of armour and the ability to use an inbuilt computer to process data from a number of sources instantly, so that the most productive decision can be made every time. This is the way board members should operate. Boards should see the strategic risk management process as evaluating what they know about every area of the business, and how reports, KPIs and benchmarks form a complete picture, and enable them to anticipate what they need to focus on. This more rounded approach should help to counter groupthink, ill-informed decisions or complacency, and lead to a more holistic approach to risk and assurance.

Peacock knew that there was a rapid pace of change in his sector. He would be leading his fellow board members to consider if they were collectively confident that they had staff who were up to date and knowledgeable. They would also be checking if their software was integrated, secure and at the cutting edge of available technology. Was it time to consider refreshing the membership of their board to ensure that there was at least one member with relevant, recent technology experience? Busy times lay ahead, but it could only result in improvements, he thought.

Bee noticed that the next session was called 'Time to Change the World'. She was feeling ready for more inspiration and motivation.

Chapter Fifteen

Outcome-based and enhanced integrated reporting

The animals were now ready for session two of step five and the thoughts of The Governor were going down well with the animals.

Bee said to Penguin: "It's great to follow up all the practical advice we've heard about the role of the NED, how we get an appointment and then actually doing the job with these sessions that help us review what we've learned and focus on issues that contribute to good governance."

"Dealing with regulators sounded scary," said Rabbit, "But The Governor's advice made perfect sense. I feel I can be more confident now about how I would work with my colleagues on a charity board to forge a good relationship with the Charity Commission."

"Social media leaves me a bit cold, "said Peacock, "I thought it was all about selfies, but I can see now that it's important to have people on boards who keep up with the latest technological advances, and that includes understanding the role and benefits of social media."

Bee and Penguin were chatting about The Governor's thoughts on succession planning and risk management.

"I appreciate the reminder that when we're analysing risks we should remember that failure to achieve objectives and realise the full potential of an organisation is as much a risk as a big catastrophe that comes out of the blue from outside our organisation and knocks us for six," said Penguin.

"It's good to see you all communicating so well with each other," said The Governor, "and, as we approach the end of our time together, we're going to continue to explore communications that impact on the role of a NED."

The TGF Zoo inhabitants were eager to hear more.

The Governor explained: "We're going to look now at how a board should be communicating with its shareholders and stakeholders. The annual report is a major opportunity for an organisation to communicate its achievements and demonstrate how it has measured up to the ideals of good governance.

"I've also got some thoughts to share with you on good governance and poor governance from interviews I have conducted with some experienced executive and non-executive directors.

"I really hope that completing the five steps will allow you to go out there and change the world."

NEDs have a golden opportunity to make a great contribution to the success of the organisations they serve. Those who want to become a NED solely for the kudos it brings – including adding it to their CV –are approaching it for the wrong reasons. If we want to change the world, we can start by promoting and contributing to good governance.

With that in mind, let's listen to what The Governor has to say about the issue of reporting along with some thoughts on good and poor governance from experienced board members.

The Governor speaks

Corporate reporting is a complex and sometimes daunting task, as it has to satisfy the needs of a variety of stakeholders. It needs to fulfil statutory disclosures, and satisfy investors, funders or the general public. Reports need to be comprehensive, but not too lengthy. They should be simple enough to read and understand, but detailed enough to provide meaningful analysis.

Organisations in the private, public and voluntary sectors are increasingly being expected to report not just on profit or surplus but also detail their impact – evidence of outcomes on and engagement with those who influence, or who are influenced by, the activities of the organisation across the wider economy, society and on the environment. The role of the annual report has evolved down the years. For many years, it has been a key source of information about companies and charities, and has included profit and loss accounts.

Today, there is an expectation that organisations will explain how they have measured up to the accepted standards of good governance. This includes how it has evaluated its performance through internal and external auditing, as well as including reporting on ethical and environmental issues.

A main principle of the UKCGC is that a board should present "a fair, balanced and understandable assessment of the company's position and prospects" (7). Thinking about production of the next annual report is an opportunity for board members to reflect on the quality of governance it has provided over the past year, and where there is room for improvement in how it is structured, as well as its processes and policies.

But in reality, how familiar is the following scenario?

It's time to start thinking about producing the annual report. The accounts department circulates the accounts and statutory notes to the executive team for comment. The narrative includes words underlined from last year's reports. The executive team is asked to include this year's figures in the spaces that have been left, and the report is sent to the board so that members can do a degree of checking and add the chair's statement. To my mind, that sounds like the incremental budgeting process of looking at last year's budget, as the baseline has already been approved, and adding a percentage.

The alternative is a zero-based budgeting approach, starting from first principles or a blank piece of paper, providing a fresh budget every year without reference to the past. My question to you is, can we adopt a similar approach to the annual report that we have with zero-based budgeting, where every element of the report is completely and comprehensively reviewed and re-evaluated? Without this fresh approach there is a likelihood that companies will fail to provide a complete picture of their prospects to the detriment of existing and potential investors, as well as other stakeholders.

Integrated reporting

Wouldn't it be great to be able to read an annual report and clearly understand how well that organisation is fulfilling its corporate objectives, how well it is governed and be able to benchmark it against other organisations? Wouldn't clear evidence of robust corporate governance, and how this is applied within the company or organisation, give greater levels of assurance?

In 2013, the International Integrated Reporting Council (IIRC) released a framework for integrated reporting following rigorous testing by businesses in 25 countries as part of a three-month global consultation. The framework established principles to govern the production of an integrated report, which would set out how the organisation's strategy, governance, performance and prospects can lead to the creation of value. The report is aimed primarily at the private sector, but it could be adapted for public sector and not-for-profit organisations.

Also of note is the 2015 report produced by the Institute of Directors (IoD) in association with the Cass Business School, called *The Great Governance Debate – Towards a Good Governance Index for Listed Companies* (49).

The Grant Thornton *UK Corporate Governance Review 2016* (50) shows that full compliance with the UKCGC was at 62% – the highest to date. But underneath this success there was evidence that a significant challenge remained for the UK's largest companies to embrace the principles of the code rather than limiting their disclosures to the minimum level acceptable.

Reviewing the FTSE 350 companies, the Grant Thornton report finds that company culture was one of the key areas still in need of attention, with only 20% of company reports giving any real insight into how companies set and embed behaviour and values throughout their organisations. The area of greatest non-compliance with the code was in respect to the balance of independent directors on the board – possibly a sign of ineffective succession planning. Reporting on shareholder engagement had fallen from 55% in 2015 to 36% in 2016.

These figures are not dissimilar in the public and voluntary sectors.

The annual requirement to produce a report – including the non-financial information or narrative reporting – provides the framework and audience for this communication. By adopting an integrated reporting approach, organisations can provide concise communication of their strategy, performance and governance.

Comply or explain

A key feature of the UKCGC is the 'comply or explain' provision. Listed companies must comply with the 18 main principles of the code and explain to shareholders how they have done so.

However, there are 55 provisions that are things that organisations can comply with or explain why they are not complying. For example, an alternative to following a provision may be justified if good governance can be achieved by other means. A condition of opting to explain non-compliance is that the reasons for it should be explained clearly and carefully to shareholders.

As a starting point, I would recommend that best practice is that all organisations should include details of how they have applied the 18 main principles of the code in their annual reports.

Typical disclosure reporting

This type of reporting is normally used to fulfil statutory requirements.

Typical disclosure reporting usually only includes the basic information necessary to show that governance has been considered, rather than it being fully integrated and expanded upon. For example, it will explicitly state compliance with relevant governance code, give a full description of the appraisal process and how the board operates, and include details of board evaluation.

Alongside this, it is common to include a biographical list of board members, details of induction and training processes, a list of committees, the number of meetings that have taken place, and a high level statement of matters reserved for the board. While informative, this is not necessarily reflective of the depth of the governance work undertaken by the organisation.

Enhancing integrated reporting

So, the question is, how can typical disclosure reporting be enhanced?

Report Leadership is a multi-stakeholder group – comprised of the Chartered Institute of Management Accountants (CIMA), PwC and Radley Yeldar – which aims to challenge established thinking on corporate reporting. It produced a report called *Corporate Governance – Simple, practical proposals for better reporting of corporate governance*, which proposes five areas that organisations should consider (51).

Using the five headings from that report, I have put together my recommendations on how standard governance reporting can be enhanced by transitioning the focus in reporting from compliance to outcomes of the governance system:

1. **Tone from the top**: The chair's statement should include a summary of his or her reflections on strategy, risk and board evaluation. This presents an opportunity to demonstrate the importance and inter-relationship of governance and leadership.
2. **How the board works as a team**: Here, emphasis should be placed on the diversity of the board, and the unique skills and experience that each board member brings rather than just presenting a list of board members' names. An important dynamic is how the executive and non-executive directors work together, and a description of this would be beneficial.
3. **The key actions of the board and its committees**: Reporting on the issues that the board and committees focused their attention on is more useful than just including a list of the terms of reference of the committees.
4. **Board effectiveness**: Make a note of the key findings identified by the evaluation process and any actions that resulted, instead of merely offering a description of the process.
5. **Communication and engagement with stakeholders**: Provide

an integrated report of the corporate integrity, social value and value for money.

Checklist for enhanced integrated reporting

An enhanced integrated report (EIR) will provide users with a better understanding of the organisation and how it is led. This detail is interwoven into the fabric of the report, negating the need for a separate governance report. An EIR may include:

- a chairman's statement to set the tone;
- the evaluation criteria linked to strategy and performance;
- achievement of the KPIs;
- the frequency of risk register reviews and key mitigations agreed;
- stakeholder feedback and investor-relations communication;
- the attendance of board members;
- the relevant skills and experience of the board;
- evidence that the evaluation process is robust, and subsequent findings;
- the outcomes of evaluations and action plans;
- evidence of progress on actions included in evaluations;
- highlighting of significant changes to governance processes during the year;
- a description of the work carried out by the audit, remuneration and nomination committees throughout the year; and
- demonstration of how the main principles of your chosen governance code are applied.

Thoughts on good and poor governance

It's always useful, I think, to listen to the views of people who have been there, done that and bought the t-shirt.

I want to share with you some of the thoughts of the people I have interviewed on what makes good and poor governance. In Chapter Nine we heard from media executive and former chairman of The FA, Greg Dyke, who said poor governance is when something goes disastrously wrong and you knew nothing about it. Good governance is when something goes disastrously wrong, but you did know about it in advance. You were warned and you did the work that was needed.

Richard Bevan, Chief Executive at the League Manager Association, told me that good governance is about having an open, transparent organisation with strong leadership and good communication. Objectives and targets are set, achieved and fully appraised afterwards. The decision-makers are accountable.

On the other hand, Richard described bad governance as what happens when individual board members are unprepared or uninformed. If they are not given accurate information, and if they don't have enough knowledge of the subject, they can't make good decisions.

The best board members, Richard said, are the ones who are good listeners, who understand the objectives of the audience and prepare really well. His final advice was to stress again how important it is to communicate really well with all the people on the board as well as the executive team.

Andy Street, the first mayor of the West Midlands Combined Authority and a former managing director of the UK retail giant John Lewis, said good governance is about having clear structures and decision-making processes. Everyone is clear on what those structures are and who is accountable for the decisions that are taken. Bad governance, he said, is when it's not clear who has the authority to take decisions, and so decisions don't get made and paralysis results. When there is no accountability, it is bad governance.

Lord Ouseley, Chair of the Kick It Out campaign and a crossbencher in the House of Lords, said that poor governance is when the organisation is not well structured and there's not clear leadership. People are not aware of the processes that are in place and the consequences of non-compliance.

He said that good governance was when people understand the rules and know what you can do within those rules, and also understand the clear objectives of their organisation.

Final thoughts on time to change the world

Good governance is an essential element of how every company functions. It is also crucial that reporting reflects governance in a way that is user-friendly, informative, and adds value to the appreciation and understanding of the effectiveness of the organisation.

Reporting shouldn't be just about compliance. Good reporting can give users a clear picture of the competency of the board, drawing out the balance of skills and expertise that serve the organisation, and documenting the work of the committees and the framework under which they operate. The reporting should highlight not only what the board evaluation processes are but what they have uncovered, how the organisation is acting on the findings and any future plans for improvement.

Peacock thought back to a few times when he had seen reporting not given the attention that it deserved. He realised that he had been guilty of assuming he knew best, and the details of how the board was structured, and the what, why, how, when and where questions had not been answered in enough detail.

Bee was also aware that this highlighted another area when she had been a bit too busy 'doing' and not as thorough in ensuring that the details of the board's work had been explained.

Penguin could see that reporting was another area where hard work had to be put in. She knew that she'd been too willing to go with the flow and not push hard enough for fear of creating conflict in the boardroom. That was going to have to change.

Rabbit was under no illusion that the whole area of being a NED was hard work, and required persistence, perseverance and preparation – plus powering through to get the job done and allow it to be seen to be done. Thank goodness he'd come on the EBM Programme!

Now the animals were facing their final session – the last chapter in step five and it was about 'wilful blindness'.

Chapter Sixteen

Risks that you want to avoid – blind spots, groupthink and wilful blindness

The final session was approaching, and Bee, Penguin, Peacock and Rabbit were reflecting on all they had learned on the EBM Programme.

They had covered so much ground across the five steps.

They had started with **why** in step one: why do you want to become a NED?

Step two had covered **what**: what does it mean to be a NED?

Step three was **how**: how do you become a NED?

Step four was another **how**: how can you be effective in the boardroom?

Step five was about putting it all into practice and listening to the key current issues around corporate governance.

The previous session on reporting had got them all thinking.

Peacock said: "I will admit that in the past I've not completely understood how the annual report can showcase what a board has achieved in a full 12 months of serving its organisation."

The others looked at Peacock and realised how far they had all come since that first session on the **6Cs** of good governance.

Bee spoke up next: "If we're busy carrying out reviews and audits – both internal and external – to continually improve, then we should be sharing that information with the public and all our stakeholders."

Rabbit looked around and said: "It's a bit surprising to me to learn that not everyone is complying with the UKCGC yet."

"But at least it's moving in the right direction," said Penguin.

"Yes," The Governor agreed, "we have seen things improve in recent years. But, sadly, things still go wrong. I've talked to you about black swan events already, but for my last session with you I want to return to the issues that can trip up even the best-run organisations.

"No board can afford to be complacent and, as you leave here, I want you to think long and hard about the pitfalls that can lie in wait for board members who start to make assumptions or take things for granted."

Most boards today follow corporate governance frameworks and comply with relevant governance codes. They may also regularly carry out strategic planning exercises and reviews. They can have robust and comprehensive risk registers and action plans that give them assurance that everything is heading in the right direction. Yet they can still make bad decisions, and their oversights can lead to corporate failures, scandals and financial crises.

Let's hear why The Governor thinks that happens and what board members can do about it.

The Governor speaks

How is it that successful leaders and the boards of mature businesses can jeopardise all those years of great achievements through an ill-informed decision? Why would they stick their heads in the sand instead of reacting to change? How can they get caught out by questionable practices within the organisation?

Reviewing the major corporate failures of recent years shows us that there were lessons that should have been learned and warning signs that should have alerted the board, but somehow these were overlooked. When you hear of yet another corporate scandal or corporate governance failure, questions such as 'Where was the board whilst this was going on?', 'What about the audit committee?' and 'What were the auditors doing?' spring to mind.

Boards regularly carry out strategic planning exercises and review the external environment. They have robust and comprehensive risk plans and mitigations that give them assurance. Boards follow stringent corporate governance frameworks and comply with relevant governance codes, and yet we still find gaps. I am not suggesting that these codes, tools and working practices are not working, nor indeed that they are not necessary, but every time I hear about a failure I think there must have been something missing.

The importance of black box thinking

Matthew Syed's book *Black Box Thinking* leads me to understand that if we can learn from our mistakes, and really study what has gone wrong when there has been a disaster, then we can put measures in place so that it doesn't happen again (52).

In the aviation industry there is a black box, as most people are aware, on every flight. This means that if there is an accident, the black box records exactly what happens. By studying the black box, investigators can ensure that the same mistakes, faults or malfunctions don't re-occur. The safety record of the aviation industry proves that this methodology really works. There's currently one accident for approximately every 2.4 million flights.

Can businesses or boards adopt this type of approach? I believe they can, and they must study and learn from corporate failures or they are doomed to repeat them.

How boards can be 'confidently wrong'

When people make a decision that they subsequently realise is wrong, there is something in human nature that encourages them to defend their decision and blame other factors for the outcome.

One example of this was a cult that predicted the end of the world on a specific date. When the day came and went, instead of this causing this doomsday cult to break up and admit they were wrong, they instead took the credit for saving the world. Boards can show a similarly stubborn attitude when it comes to defending their poor decisions and explaining away the warning signs that they missed. I believe that the more successful an organisation is, and the more accomplished and mature the board is, the more difficult it is for the board members to consider their own vulnerabilities.

Boards, in my experience, can be 'confidently wrong'. By this I mean that they firmly believe that what they're doing is in the best interests of the organisation, and they convince themselves that if they are professional, and if they monitor and scrutinise well, then all will be fine.

The problem is that sometimes boards are wrong; sometimes they don't have the answers, and sometimes they don't anticipate and deal with major issues. They are so confident that what they are doing is right that they don't even recognise the option that they could be wrong; this is what I describe as being 'confidently wrong'.

Leaders and boards afflicted by being 'confidently wrong' have a tendency to think of any mistake as a one-off, a unique incident or a black swan (so-called because of its rarity). Worst of all they don't accept that there was anything they could have done differently. The black box thinking that I mentioned earlier, will not work because board members don't recognise that there are lessons they can learn.

When data comes in, which conflicts with what they originally thought to be correct and provides evidence of a flaw in their strategy, they fail to adapt and become more rigid in their thinking, pursuing the original flawed strategy even more vehemently. Why do I say this? Well, there was the South Sea Bubble, there was the Tulip Bubble, there was the Dot.com Bubble, and more recently the Housing Bubble, and what we know is that bubbles burst. But how many times have we found that organisations just don't learn from these crashes? I could mention Barings Bank. I could mention Société Générale. I could mention Union Bank of Switzerland (UBS) or the names synonymous with these failings: Nick Leeson, James Kerviel, Kweku Adoboli or Bernie Madoff.

I can guarantee that, although we have enough black box thinking to ensure that we never have another rogue trader or we never see another bubble, there will be some sort of crisis brewing even now.

Beware these potential pitfalls for boards

There are three areas that boards need to be aware of if they want to avoid their own corporate crash.

The first one is arrogance and the outcome of that is groupthink. Before we discuss groupthink in a bit more detail it would be useful to note how arrogance can be defined. A general understanding would be classified as some form of offensive display of superiority or self-importance with a display of pride. We will examine the tendency for boards to adopt an arrogant stance and the challenges that this brings. Arrogant board behaviour can be typified by the attitude of 'That's how we do things.'

The second area is ignorance and the outcome of that is blind spots. A wider definition of ignorance is a lack of knowledge, lack of learning or lack of information. We will take a deeper look into how being unaware of what's going on is no excuse for a board.

The third area is stubbornness and the outcome of that is wilful blindness. Stubbornness is generally understood as an individual being unreasonably and obstructively determined to persevere or prevail. We will explore why boards sometimes find it difficult to change their opinions and doggedly follow a particular detrimental path.

There we have it: groupthink, blind spots and wilful blindness as part of our three-pronged attack on 'confidently wrong' boards.

What is groupthink?

Research psychologist Irving Janis is most famous for his theory of groupthink, which describes the systematic errors made by groups when making collective decisions. He defines it as when "the members of a group striving for unanimity override their motivation to realistically appraise alternative courses of action". The importance, he says, is that "this leads to a deterioration of mental efficiency, reality testing and moral judgement that results from group pressures" (53).

A lot of examples of groupthink have occurred in situations connected with war and international conflict, such as the Bay of Pigs and Pearl Harbour. Another example was the Watergate scandal during the presidency of Richard Nixon.

In a corporate setting, boards that are susceptible to groupthink make bad decisions because they try to conform rather than challenge. Dr John Carver says "boards are incompetent groups of competent individuals". Just because the individuals are competent doesn't mean the group, in our case the board of directors, will be.

Groups do have the potential to be smarter than individuals, as James Surowiecki notes in his book *The Wisdom of the Crowds*. It is when we get to a place where the board believes that it is always right and always wise that we have a problem.

There are three types of groupthink:

1. **Over-estimation of the group**:

Janis refers to an 'illusion of invulnerability' shared by almost all of a group. The board, or leaders, suffer from self-delusion because they believe that the business is doing well, it always has done well and it always will do well. This leads them to make misjudgements through over-confidence.

2. **Closed-mindedness**:

The board rationalises past decisions rather than reconsidering any assumptions. The members ignore information, underestimate competition or get their position in the market place completely wrong, and close their minds to any alternatives.

3. **Pressure to conform**:

Pressure from within the group, or from a skilled chair, can silence dissenting views or make those with an alternative point of view feel uncomfortable. This can be done by intimating that there is pressure to complete the agenda on time, asking the chair to declare there is no time to take any more comments or saying 'We're all agreed on this one, aren't we?'

What is a blind spot?

We know that when we are driving there are always things that are out of sight, despite having a rear view mirror and side mirrors. In order to manoeuvre our vehicles safely, we sometimes need to move our heads to see what is in our blind spot.

In the boardroom, we can become ignorant of what is going on if we fall foul of one of three types of blind spot. The first one is a blinkered way of thinking that stops us seeing those rare but catastrophic events (the black swans) coming our way. I believe that organisations and boards should be like fire fighters: ready and waiting to respond when problems arise.

In the classic management book by Spencer Johnson, *Who Moved My Cheese? An Amazing Way to Deal with Change in Your Work and in Your Life*, we're reminded that the cheese won't always be there and we need to make sure that we are prepared for that eventuality (54). Andy Grove, CEO of Intel Corporation, said it this way: "Sooner or later, something fundamental in your business world will change" (31). Although we can't see what's coming, we should be in a perpetual state of readiness for those black-swan-type events and avoid complacency.

The second type of blind spot is an erroneous way of thinking, which relies on past experiences that may not help us to predict what will happen in the future. This type of thinking will not necessarily take your organisation to where it needs to go. One example of this is **sector arrogance**. Boards may assume that how things are done and what is achieved in their sector is applicable to other sectors. For example, an overall 80% customer-satisfaction ranking may be acceptable in one sector, whereas another sector expects 90%. Customers and consumers expect the same level of service regardless of what sector they are in.

Boards need to understand that the organisations that they lead operate in a global environment. Consumer expectations spread across industries, sectors and global jurisdictions. If any of them set a particular standard, then that standard is expected by the consumer regardless of which organisation they are dealing with. Organisations can no longer say 'this is the way we do it in our sector'. That type of sector arrogance will cause the competition to overtake you and sometimes render your organisation impotent.

Another example of erroneous thinking is **cultural myopia**. People may be saying that your service is not good or you're not treating customers in the right way. As we saw in the UK with retail group Sports Direct, there may be accusations that employees are being treated poorly. But the board and its executives may think 'we are making money, we are okay', and they don't see it as a problem.

It was back in the 1980s that the book *In Search Of Excellence*, by Robert Waterman and Tom Peters, took an in-depth look at the impact of culture on strategy (55). When an organisation adopts a culture that is critical of its stakeholders, whether that is beneficiaries, customers or shareholders, and when that organisation is being told that it is not as good as it thinks it is, then that board is suffering from a cultural blind spot.

The third type of blind spot is when leaders and boards try to collectively manage rather than lead the organisation. This happens when boards try to execute where their role should be to direct and control. Boards that get themselves involved in the operational detail and interfere with the role of the management team create innumerable problems, and leave the organisation without the appropriate leadership that the boards are in place to deliver.

What is wilful blindness?

We are all aware of the phrase 'love is blind'. We tend not to see faults or weaknesses in our loved ones. We are literally blind to them sometimes.

There is a real problem for boards, however, when they're wilfully blind. How many executives in the entertainment industry, senior church figures or, more recently, people in the football industry were really unaware of incidents of abuse? Did people really not know what was going on or did they turn a blind eye? Worse than that, did some people attempt a cover-up when activities were discovered? In the private sector, were executives in the banking sector completely unsighted about what was really going on before the financial crisis that eventually exploded? Writer Margaret Heffernan talks extensively about the concept and principles of wilful blindness in her book of the same name, which I highly recommend (56).

There is a parable in the Bible that talks about the concept of having eyes but not perceiving. Wilful blindness by a board isn't about not seeing because of blind spots – it's about seeing and ignoring, or seeing and not accepting what you're seeing.

Isn't it the case that sometimes inappropriate practices, behaviours and standards are accepted because despite them, certain performance indicators are met? Dare I mention, for instance, the vehicle emissions manipulations, misleading/fraudulent profit calculations in the food sector or the traders who colluded for years to rig Libor, the banks' lending rate. It is hard to believe that boards weren't aware of some of these issues before the scandals broke, but if they didn't know they are equally responsible. Ignorance is no excuse for a board.

How can we improve board behaviours?

Traditional governance models are very good for the compliance side of things. Boards need to have procedures in place and to comply with a governance code. Members of a board need to have the right skills and experience on paper; they need to follow the organisation's strategy and have risk plans in place. But, even with all that structure and discipline, boards need to move to the next level of governance understanding.

So, how do we see better? How do we ensure that we don't miss what's in our blind spots?

How do we make the best use of the talents within our board, instead of being victims of our own self-delusion?

In TGF's governance framework, we first look at compliance drivers, i.e. the structures required to run an organisation effectively. Next we look at the composition and skills of the board, and finally we examine how they collectively execute their role.

That collective performance, or performance drivers, has to start with total transparency of reporting. There needs to be an integrated reporting approach that includes corporate integrity, commercial sustainability and openness. Another element of performance drivers are the impact that the organisation has across its many stakeholders and the boundaries within which it operates. Finally, board performance is directly linked to the behaviour of the board members, individually and collectively.

What is required, once compliance basics are met, is what I'm calling insight. Board members need more than normal individual intelligence; they need collective intelligence. One and one doesn't always make two; sometimes it makes three. Unfortunately, on most boards one and one actually makes less than two. You can have very intelligent people, but when you put them together they become dysfunctional.

What I want to get across is that diversity on boards is about more than race, gender and age – although that is important for many reasons. Diversity is also about having the right blend of functional skills (lawyers, marketing experts, financial professionals, etc.) and it is also about different life and cultural experiences. Bringing that collective intelligence together gives collective wisdom that is almost intuitive, so you can predict where something's not quite right. If a black swan event happens, a board with collective intelligence and intuitive governance can predict it, or react very quickly.

Boards must get to a place of collective wisdom, and to do this they need collective intelligence. This means a diversity of experience with a comprehensive, robust and varied approach to gathering collective intelligence, which can then be applied appropriately to a governance framework. Diversity of thinking comes from having diversity in three areas: the styles of approach to decision-making or problem-solving; the core disciplines; and race, gender and cultural diversity. But the model of considering compliance drivers and performance drivers in TGF's governance framework isn't sufficient alone to deal with a 'confidently wrong' board.

Compliance drivers are analogous with the oversight functions of the board. It is clear, however, that governance is more than compliance, so, as you move from conforming to performing, the drivers are now more about foresight functions than oversight. We move from that compliance role into a more strategic role. In order to effectively deal with an increasingly volatile, uncertain, complex and ambiguous business world, in order to anticipate the unpredictable and to be able to manage disruptive influences, we need more generative forms of governance.

Final thoughts on wilful blindness

Boards should be a group of individuals working together, comfortably relying on each other's unique skills, experience and knowledge; using that collective intelligence to predict and to evaluate disruptive risks and opportunities; to identify areas of growth and development; and to ensure the organisation is protected from its own success. We move from oversight to foresight to insight and from compliance to performance to intuition.

One thing the four animals were all agreed on was that no one wanted failure to happen on their watch. The final session on wilful blindness had been a wake-up call. The animals would be leaving the EBM Programme with renewed determination to improve their behaviour.

Peacock knew there was no room for arrogance and assumptions in a boardroom. Every old dog (or, in this case, bird) can be taught new tricks, and Peacock was returning to his boardroom with a new humility, and a willingness to listen and learn.

Penguin knew that it was impossible to be everyone's friend all the time and still be an effective board member. She was going to work on scrutinising and challenging to avoid allowing anything to slip by her that could have serious consequences for the organisation that she loved.

Bee knew that strategy and planning was a vital part of her role – not just filling every hour with activity that didn't always have a purpose. She remembered the passion she had for her role and how important the organisation she served was to its customers. She could work on her patience, and her preparation and communication skills, and that chair role she wanted could be hers in the future.

Rabbit was so pleased to have completed the programme. He knew that a little bit of insecurity would always be with him, but he was going to recalibrate it, and use it to focus on what he really wanted to do and the impact he wanted to have. A little bit of nerves would keep him on his toes, he felt.

It had been a great journey for the four animals from the TGF Zoo and The Governor was proud of their progress. He was confident that all of them – from the inexperienced Rabbit to the highly qualified Peacock, now understood more about the importance and benefits of good governance.

In his book *The Fish Rots From The Head*, Bob Garratt says "An organisation's success or failure depends on the performance of its board, yet the majority of directors have no special training for their role and are unsure about quite what it entails." (57)

The Governor's EBM Programme was all about changing that. As his four latest graduates stepped back into business life, it was time to start the next programme with a new cohort...

To find out how you can book your place on the next EBM Programme, where you will learn more about what Bee, Peacock, Penguin and Rabbit have experienced on their journey, meet other members of The TGF Zoo and discover how to maintain effectiveness in the boardroom, please visit www.effectiveboardmember.co.uk today!

"Now'" said The Governor, "can you tell me which animal you think represents a highly effective board member?"

References

1. Drucker PF. The Effective Executive. London: Routledge; 2011. 167 p.

2. Karinthy F. Chain-Links [Internet]. 1929 [cited 2017 Jul 9]. Available from: https://djjr-courses.wdfiles.com/local--files/soc180%3Akarinthy-chain-links/Karinthy-Chain-Links_1929.pdf

3. Tyndale House Publishers. Holy Bible: New Living Translation. Wheaton, Ill.: Tyndale House Publishers; 2004.

4. Darling A. Companies Act 2006 [Internet]. 2006. Available from: http://www.legislation.gov.uk/ukpga/2006/46/contents

5. Robinson HSFL-J, Laurence D, Gunson C. Directors' duties in the UAE - what are the potential personal liabilities? | Lexology [Internet]. [cited 2017 Jul 9]. Available from: http://www.lexology.com/library/detail.aspx?g=17cdb1a1-aef2-4d10-b448-7ad1fa0e24b8

6. UK Government. Charity trustee: what's involved (CC3a) - GOV.UK [Internet]. [cited 2017 Jul 9]. Available from: https://www.gov.uk/guidance/charity-trustee-whats-involved

7. Financial Reporting Council. UK Corporate Governance Code [Internet]. 2016 [cited 2017 Jul 13]. Available from: https://www.frc.org.uk/Our-Work/Codes-Standards/Corporate-governance/UK-Corporate-Governance-Code.aspx

8. Tzu S. The Art of War. 1 edition. Chiron Academic Press; 2015. 108 p.

9. Wilson P, Bates S. The Essential Guide to Managing Small Business Growth. 1 edition. Wiley; 2008. 316 p.

10. Drucker PF. Concept of the Corporation. New edition. New York: John Day Co; 1972.

11. Levitt T. Marketing Myopia. Harvard Business Review Press; 2008. 100 p.

12. Chandler. Strategy and Structure: Chapters in the History of the

American Industrial Enterprise. Reprint edition. Cambridge, Mass: MIT Press; 1974. 480 p.

13. Collins J. Good to Great and the Social Sectors: A Monograph to Accompany Good to Great. London: Random House Business; 2006. 48 p.

14. Kim WC, Mauborgne R, Mauborgne RA. Blue Ocean Strategy, Expanded Edition: How to Create Uncontested Market Space and Make the Competition Irrelevant. Expanded edition. Harvard Business Review Press; 2014. 320 p.

15. Taleb NN. The Black Swan: the Impact of the Highly Improbable. London: Penguin; 2008.

16. Johnson G, Scholes K, Whittington R. Exploring Strategy. Harlow: Financial Times Prentice Hall; 2011.

17. Morrison A, Wensley R. Boxing up or boxed in?: A short history of the Boston Consulting Group share/growth matrix. Journal of Marketing Management. 1991;7(2):105–129.

18. Ansoff HI. Strategies for Diversification. Harvard Business Review. 1957 Sep;35(5):113–24.

19. Higgs D. Review of the role and effectiveness of non-executive directors [Internet]. 2003 [cited 2017 Aug 14]. Available from: http://www.bis.gov.uk/files/file23012.pdf

20. Rath T, Clifton DO. How full is your bucket? positive strategies for work and life. 1. ed. New York, NY: Gallup; 2004. 127 p.

21. Nolan M. The 7 principles of public life - GOV.UK [Internet]. [cited 2017 Jul 9]. Available from: https://www.gov.uk/government/publications/the-7-principles-of-public-life/the-7-principles-of-public-life--2

22. UK Government. Terms of reference - Committee on Standards in Public Life - GOV.UK [Internet]. 2013 [cited 2017 Jul 13]. Available from: https://www.gov.uk/government/organisations/the-committee-on-standards-in-public-life/about/terms-of-reference

23. the governance forum - YouTube [Internet]. [cited 2017 Jul 9]. Available from: https://www.youtube.com/

24. George K. The Little Book of Governance. 2nd edition. Muir L, editor. Birmingham: The Governance Forum; 2015. 85 p.

25. Cadbury A. The Financial Aspects of Corporate Performance [Internet]. 1992. Available from: https://www.icaew.com/-/media/corporate/files/library/subjects/corporate-governance/financial-aspects-of-corporate-governance.ashx?la=en

26. Smith & Williamson. Smith & Williamson Power 100 [Internet]. Fresh Business Thinking. [cited 2017 Jul 13]. Available from: http://www.freshbusinessthinking.com/smith-williamson-power-100/

27. Kotter JP. Leading Change, With a New Preface by the Author. 1R edition. Harvard Business Review Press; 2012. 220 p.

28. Kotter JP, Cohen DS. The Heart of Change: Real-Life Stories of How People Change Their Organizations. 1 edition. Harvard Business Review Press; 2012. 214 p.

29. Hodge C. FTSE304 Corporate Governance Review [Internet]. Grant Thornton; 2013 [cited 2017 Aug 14]. Available from: https://www.grantthornton.global/globalassets/1.-member-firms/united-kingdom/pdf/publication/2013/ftse-350-corporate-governance-review-2013.pdf

30. Financial Reporting Council. Guidance on Board Effectiveness [Internet]. 2011. [cited 2017 Aug 14] Available from: https://www.frc.org.uk/Our-Work/Publications/Corporate-Governance/Guidance-on-Board-Effectiveness.pdf

31. Grove AS. Only the Paranoid Survive: How to Exploit the Crisis Points That Challenge Every Company. 1st Currency Pbk. Ed edition. New York Toronto: Crown Business; 1999. 240 p.

32. NHS Leadership Academy. The Healthy NHS Board NHS Leadership Academy| NHS Leadership Academy [Internet]. 2013 [cited 2014 Mar 15]. Available from: http://www.leadershipacademy.nhs.uk/discover/the-healthy-nhs-board/

33. Garratt B. Thin On Top: Why Corporate Governance Matters and How to Measure and Improve Board Performance. 2Rev Ed edition. Yarmouth, ME: Nicholas Brealey Publishing; 2006. 260 p.

34. Underwood F, Kane S, Appleby M. Cosmopolitan Housing Group: lessons learned [Internet]. Altair. 2014 [cited 2017 Jul 15]. Available from: http://altairltd.co.uk/2014/06/cosmopolitan-housing-group-lessons-learned/

35. Kelly C. The Kelly Review [Internet]. 2014 [cited 2017 Jul 13]. Available from: https://www.co-operative.coop/investors/kelly-review

36. Myners P. Institutional Investment in the United Kingdom: A Review [Internet]. 2001 [cited 2017 Aug 22]. Available from: http://uksif.org/wp-content/uploads/2012/12/MYNERS-P.-2001.-Institutional-Investment-in-the-United-Kingdom-A-Review.pdf

37. Regan D. Housing Corporation welcomes Ujima report [Internet]. Housing Excellence. 2008 [cited 2017 Jul 15]. Available from: http://www.housingexcellence.co.uk/news/housing-corporation-welcomes-ujima-report-233231

38. Home and Communities Agency. Homes and Communities Agency - GOV.UK [Internet]. 2017 [cited 2017 Jul 15]. Available from: https://www.gov.uk/government/organisations/homes-and-communities-agency

39. Bull S, National Housing Federation. Excellence in governance: code for members and good practice guidance. London: National Housing Federation; 2010.

40. Burrowes K. PwC: Over-regulation and cyber risk top CEOs' list of threats to banking & capital markets growth - Press room [Internet]. 2015 [cited 2017 Jul 13]. Available from: http://pwc.blogs.com/press_room/2015/02/pwc-over-regulation-and-cyber-risk-top-ceos-list-of-threats-to-banking-capital-markets-growth.html

41. Davies M. Women on Boards [Internet]. UK Government; Available from: https://www.gov.uk/government/uploads/system/uploads/attachment_data/file/31480/11-745-women-on-boards.pdf

42. Chan SP. Vince Cable: number of women leading UK boardrooms 'pitifully small'. 2014 Dec 14 [cited 2017 Aug 21]; Available from: http://www.telegraph.co.uk/finance/globalbusiness/11292838/Vince-Cable-number-of-women-leading-UK-boardrooms-pitifully-small.html

43. Joseph I. Why small charities can benefit from investing in trustee recruitment. The Guardian [Internet]. 2013 Apr 29; Available from: https://www.theguardian.com/voluntary-sector-network/2013/apr/29/small-charities-trustee-recruitment

44. Kollewe J, Hickey S. A third of boardroom positions should be held by women, UK firms told. The Guardian [Internet]. 2015 Oct 29; Available from: https://www.theguardian.com/business/2015/oct/29/a-third-of-boardroom-positions-should-be-held-by-women-uk-firms-told

45. Parker J. A Report into the Ethnic Diversity of UK Boards [Internet]. The Parker Review Committee; 2016 [cited 2017 Jul 13]. Available from: http://www.ey.com/Publication/vwLUAssets/A_Report_into_the_Ethnic_Diversity_of_UK_Boards/%24FILE/Beyond%20One%20by%2021%20PDF%20Report.pdf

46. Institute of Risk Managers. Cyber risk [Internet]. Cyber risk and risk management. [cited 2017 Aug 14]. Available from: https://www.theirm.org/knowledge-and-resources/thought-leadership/cyber-risk/

47. Rushe D. The Interview revenge hack cost Sony just $15m. The Guardian [Internet]. 2015 Feb 4; Available from: https://www.theguardian.com/film/2015/feb/04/guardians-peace-revenge-hack-sony-finances-unscathed

48. Nanterme P. Digital disruption has only just begun [Internet]. World Economic Forum. 2016 [cited 2017 Jul 13]. Available from: https://www.weforum.org/agenda/2016/01/digital-disruption-has-only-just-begun/

49. Institute of Directors, Cass Business School. The Great Governance Debate - Towards a Good Governance Index for Listed Companies [Internet]. 2015 [cited 2017 Jul 13]. Available from: https://www.iod.com/Portals/0/PDFs/Campaigns%20and%20Reports/Corporate%20Governance/IoD%20Good%20Governance%20Index%202015.pdf?ver=2016-08-31-153353-510

50. Lowe S. UK Corporate Governance Review 2016 highlights [Internet]. Grant Thornton UK LLP. 2016 [cited 2017 Jul 13]. Available from: http://www.grantthornton.co.uk/en/insights/uk-corporate-governance-review-2016-highlights/

51. Report Leadership. Corporate Governance – Simple, practical proposals for better reporting of corporate governance [Internet]. [cited 2017 Aug 21]. Available from: http://www.cimaglobal.com/Documents/Thought_leadership_docs/Governance/Report-Leadership-Corporate-Governance-Report.pdf

52. Syed M. Black Box Thinking: Marginal Gains and the Secrets of High Performance. 01 edition. John Murray; 2016. 352 p.

53. Janis IL. Groupthink: psychological studies of policy decisions and fiascoes. 2. ed., [Nachdr.]. Boston: Wadsworth; 2013. 351 p.

54. Johnson DS. Who Moved My Cheese: An Amazing Way to Deal with Change in Your Work and in Your Life. Reprinted Ed edition. London: Vermilion; 1999. 96 p.

55. Peters TJ, Waterman R. In Search of Excellence: Lessons from America's Best-run Companies. Harper; 1982.

56. Heffernan M. Wilful Blindness: Why We Ignore the Obvious. UK ed. edition. Simon & Schuster UK; 2011. 400 p.

57. Garratt B. The Fish Rots From The Head: The Crisis in our Boardrooms: Developing the Crucial Skills of the Competent Director. Main edition. Profile Books; 2010. 320 p.

58. Leblanc, R. & Gillies, J. Inside the Boardroom: How Boards Really Work and the Coming Revolution in Corporate Governance, Main Edition. Wiley; 2005. 138 p.

KEY TOPIC INDEX

Step Three – How to get an Appointment

A NOTE FROM A FRIEND

Karl has inspired hundreds of individuals of all ages during his time working in both business and the community. An aspect of his background that is not known more widely is his passion to serve and give back to the community, whether that be the business community, his local neighbourhood or sometimes in a wider, international context. You are naturally drawn to his inspiring and charismatic style of delivery, and you will experience this in this book with Karl as The Governor. In 2004, his contribution was justly recognised when he was awarded an MBE. Not only is Karl an advocate for governance, but he is a true man of the people.

Karl would be the first to tell you that if you want to change anything, you need to influence leadership, and this is how his business and community values tie up. He practises what he preaches and firmly believes that change happens one individual (be that a board member or mentee) at a time, and that, during this process, you have the potential to impact others in ways you could not imagine. A real testament to him are the thousands of individuals who have been impacted by The Governor and the impact that they now make in their own right. Right at the forefront of his discourse on influence, however, you won't find the captains of industry who he has mentored or coached but an individual who he encountered during his work in the community. Imagining this, when he has delivered programmes, courses and training to CEOs of international and global entities, government ministers, head teachers, dames, knights and such like, may be hard, but Karl is truly one of a kind.

Action is something Karl does and speaking to him, it is the story of one young man from inner city Birmingham who was 15 when he met and began mentoring him that helps you to understand his vision and passion.

Duane Henry is that young man, who now lives in Los Angeles and is a lead actor and a star of *NCIS*, one of the most watched TV shows globally, in which he plays Clayton Reeves – and, when not in character, is known to attribute a large part of his success to Karl's inspirational and innovative teaching methods, his mentoring, and his focus and drive. A testament to his consistency, you will find that all of these principles are applied on the EBM Programmes and, along with the methods outlined in this book, will help anyone to be a great success in any boardroom, anywhere in the world. Not many people can claim to get excited about corporate governance, or even get 'tingly' as Karl puts it, but I know that this book and his programmes have the ability to do just that, and, in doing that, he is set to make a difference by changing the world one board member at a time.

Cyrille Regis MBE
Former England International Footballer

ABOUT THE AUTHOR

Karl George MBE is an international governance consultant, author, feature writer, visiting professor, Association of Chartered Certified Accountants (ACCA) fellow and award winning businessman, with over 25 years' combined experience in accountancy, business and corporate governance. As managing director of the governance forum, Karl now works with CEOs, boards and senior executives across the private, public and voluntary sectors, delivering exceptional insight for corporate governance solutions.

His work in the field with hundreds of organisations and thousands of individuals has led to him develop a unique governance framework and kitemark that was endorsed by the late Sir Adrian Cadbury. The framework formed the foundation of the university-accredited Effective Board Member (EBM) Programmes, which Karl delivers and has licensed to partners including PwC. The programmes are now delivered in six countries across the world, including the Middle East and the Caribbean, and have had more than 500 graduates.

This pioneering series of programmes, which have been featured by the BBC and The Telegraph, are also delivered in partnership with the PFA and The FA, and over the last four years has recruited and trained almost 80 current and ex-professional footballers, coaches and those working in the sport, mainly from BAME backgrounds. Not only has he created a pool of board-ready, high profile candidates, over half have secured board placements or appointments, changing representation within the higher echelons of the game.

A seasoned non-executive himself, Karl's expertise in governance combined with his qualified accountant status makes him a sought-after board member, both locally and internationally. Karl is well respected in the business community and was one of the founders of the Young Directors Forum at the Institute of Directors (IoD). He is a founding member of the Association of Corporate Governance Practitioners (ACGP), the only international professional body for cross-sector governance practitioners.

Karl's passion to serve has seen him pioneer a number of other initiatives over the last two decades. He started the first international chapter of 100 Black Men, a mentoring programme with over 10,000 members in the US. As a Reach Role Model, Karl was one of only 20 individuals from across the UK selected to deliver this government-led, national activity aimed at raising the aspirations of men from BAME backgrounds. More recently, Karl pioneered the national Diversity in the Boardroom Campaign, which is encouraging organisations to pledge to improve diversity in boardrooms beyond the FTSE.

The community awards and business accolades he has received include investiture as MBE for services to the community in 2004.

OTHER BOOKS BY KARL GEORGE MBE

Most People Only Try, I Make Sure

A look at the nature of business success and seven simple strategies to help you achieve it

The Little Book of Governance

Boards Behaving Badly